BASIC:

A Programmed Text

BASIC:

A Programmed Text

SEYMOUR HIRSCH

General Electric Company,

MELVILLE PUBLISHING COMPANY

LOS ANGELES, CALIFORNIA

DEDICATED TO MY MOTHER
ELLA

Library of Congress Cataloging in Publication Data:

Hirsch, Seymour C
 BASIC: a programmed text.

 Includes index.
 1. Basic (Computer program language)--Programmed
instruction. I. Title
QA76.73.B3H57   001.6'424   75-6806
ISBN 0-471-40045-9

Printed in the United States of America

10 9 8 7 6 5 4 3 2 1

PREFACE

This book has been designed to be a self-teaching manual in the BASIC programming language. Using the "programmed text" approach, a student should be able to go through the frames in this book in approximately 8 hours of self-study.

Special efforts have been expended to help make this book easy and pleasant to read. The use of technical terms has been deliberately avoided. Attempts have been made to present examples in an easy to understand and useful manner.

If the student has a terminal and is authorized to practice using a distant computer, he should try out the examples given in this book. By actual "hands-on" experience, the student will reinforce his knowledge and learn at a faster pace.

To the Student

You may find that this book is unlike any other you are accustomed to. There are no long, wordy paragraphs to wade through. There are no tedious explanations. Instead you will find short "frames" that give a unit of knowledge, then ask you to take part.

You will not simply take a passive part in your BASIC education. You will be taking an active part by responding to questions that are asked. If your answers are correct, you will be told where to proceed next; if your answers are incorrect, you will be told why then given further directions concerning where to proceed.

Some of the questions in the frames are very simple. Some more difficult. Some may bring a smile. In any event, you will find that progress can be made at a very rapid rate. Some students will take longer than others. This is no problem, since each person proceeds at the rate that is best for him. When you have completed this book, you will know how to program in BASIC.

There is very little writing involved. Read through the frames, then answer the questions. It's OK to have a scratch pad at your side for some occasional figuring.

You will find that each frame is numbered. And each frame text is followed by several frame number and answer combinations. Select the best answer and turn to the frame indicated. When no answer is required the text will tell you which frame is next.

At the conclusion of each section, answer the questions and do the problems in the quizzes found near the back of the book. Then check your responses with the answers also located there.

Please proceed now to Frame 1 and follow directions. Good luck.

CONTENTS

viii

SECTION I

INTRODUCTION

FRAME 1

The power of a large-scale computer is as near to you as your telephone. Once you have been properly validated as a timesharing user, you may pick up the phone, dial the distant computer, and begin solving your problem. We'll give you the details of how this is actually done in the next few frames.

Would you agree that if you know a computer's telephone number you may begin using that computer at once?

2   Yes

3   No

4   Yes, if you have a good credit rating.

FRAME 2

Sorry, your answer, Yes, is not correct.
It's not enough to know the computer's
phone number. You must also be a validated
user. This means that you must first contact
the organization that sells timesharing
services and make the proper arrangements.
This fact should cause you no concern. Go
see the people; They'll be pleased to see
you.

Please go to Frame 3.

FRAME 3

No is the correct answer. You must be validated as a user. This is no problem since
many service bureaus offer computer time on
a shared-time basis. When you are validated
as a user, you will be given the computer's
phone number and a personal identification
code (ID).

To use the computer you must sit at a type-
writer-like terminal, then pick up the phone
and dial the computer's number. When the
computer responds with a high-pitched tone,
you must place the receiver into a cradle
especially installed on your terminal for
this purpose. The computer then types a
message on your terminal. It asks for your:

5　Name

6　Identification code (ID)

7　Social security number

FRAME 4

You should have a good credit rating, of course, just on general principles. But this isn't the answer we wanted.

Please go back to Frame 1. Read it carefully, then answer the question again.

FRAME 5

The computer is not really interested in your
name or your social security number. The
most important item of information you can
give the computer is your identification code
(ID). The computer checks this code against
the list of validated users. If your code is
in that list, you are permitted to go to the
next step; if it isn't you are politely, but
firmly, refused access to the computer.

To see what you do in response to a request
for ID, please go to Frame 6.

FRAME 6

Your identification code (ID) is the correct
answer.

Now you must do some typing. You type your
ID and wait for the computer's next message.
You and the computer are now engaged in a
conversation. The computer types a message
or question and you respond; then it types
another message or question and you respond
again. Because of the conversational procedure, this type of computer usage is referred to as "conversational timesharing."

Conversational timesharing means that you
and the computer engage in a:

8 Conversation

9 Battle of wits

FRAME 7

No, the computer has no interest in your
social security number. It's not interested
in your name either. The computer wants
your identification code (ID). Please read
Frame 3 again and then proceed from there.

FRAME 8

The correct answer is conversation.

After checking your ID and finding it to be valid, the computer requests the name of the programming language you intend to use. Besides BASIC, FORTRAN, and ALGOL, many other languages are available. In this text we will discuss only the BASIC language. Therefore, when the computer types

SYSTEM?

You respond

10 FORTRAN

11 ALGOL

12 BASIC

FRAME 9

No, you do not engage in a battle of wits
with the computer. The computer is not an
opponent. Tell the computer what you want
it to do and the computer will obey. The
correct response is "conversation." Be careful, though, you must tell the computer
exactly what you want it to do. If you give
the computer wrong instructions, all you will
receive is wrong answers.

Please go to Frame 8.

FRAME 10

FORTRAN is a computer programming language
and is available on many timesharing services,
but this book is dedicated to the topic of
BASIC. The answer we were looking for was
BASIC.

Please go to Frame 12.

FRAME 11

ALGOL is a computer programming language and is available on many timesharing services. But this book is not about ALGOL or FORTRAN, it's about BASIC. You should have entered BASIC.

Please go to Frame 12.

FRAME 12

BASIC is correct. Next, the computer will
want to know whether you would like to run
a program which you developed in the past or
if you want to create a new program. Suppose
you want to create a brand new program.
When the computer types:

OLD OR NEW?

you should reply:

13   OLD

14   NEW

15   BASIC

FRAME 13

No, OLD is not correct. Read the frame again.
You want to create a new program. You wouldn't
type OLD if you meant NEW.

Please go back to Frame 12 and give a different
answer.

FRAME 14

Yes, the answer is NEW.

In addition to the word NEW or OLD, the computer will want a program name. You may give it a name such as:

NEW TEST

or

OLD ABRUS

In the first example, you will make up a name containing up to six characters. In the second example, you are asking the computer to give you a program having the name shown that you created at some earlier time.

Can you guess what would happen if you type OLD or NEW without giving a program name?

16   The computer will stop.

17   The computer will select a standard name.

18   The computer will ask for a name.

FRAME 15

No, you're making this harder than it should
be. The computer types OLD OR NEW? The
question is simple, requiring a simple answer
selected from the words OLD or NEW.

Please go back to Frame 12 and give a different
response.

FRAME 16

Your answer that the computer will stop is
not a good guess. The computer sees that
you have not given a name and simply asks
for it. The computer types

FILE NAME?

and you respond. If this is a new program,
you must make up a name containing no more
than six characters. If this is an old program, you must provide the name that you
gave the program when you first created it.

Please go now to Frame 18.

FRAME 17

Your answer that the computer will select a
standard name is a good guess, but unfortunately is not correct. If the system really
gave a standard name, you might wind up with
several programs all having that same name.
Actually, the computer asks for the name.

Please go to Frame 16 to see what our comments
would have been had you replied that the
computer would stop. Then continue from that
frame.

FRAME 18

The computer does indeed ask for a name.
There are two things to remember when you
give a program a name. First, the name may
contain up to six characters made up of letters and/or digits. Second, the name should
remind you of what the program does.

Suppose for example that you want to enter a
program which generates random numbers. What
would you most likely call it?

19   RANDNUMS

20   RNDNUM

21   BENSON

FRAME 19

Your answer of RANDNUMS is not correct because there are too many characters in the
name. The maximum number of characters is 6.

Please go back to Frame 18 and give a different response.

FRAME 20

Yes, RNDNUM is a good selection because the name reminds you of what the program does. The name RANDNUMS might seem to be a good selection, but it is too long.

The computer now types

READY

The message means that the "sign on" procedure has been completed and you may begin typing your program. When you request the assistance of a computer in solving a problem, you must tell the computer what to do every step of the way. It's as if you had a giant clerk at your command. When you want the clerk to do something for you, you must tell him what to do. It's the same with a computer. When you want it to complete a solution to a problem, you must tell the computer

22 What time you want the job done.

23 What you want it to do.

FRAME 21

The name BENSON has probably been selected
because it is the name of the user. You,
perhaps. But the name doesn't help remind
you what the program does.

Please go back to Frame 18 to see if you can
select a more appropriate name.

FRAME 22

No, your response is not correct. When you
want to obtain the answers to a problem, you
must tell the computer what you want it to do.
There is no need to tell the computer when
you want the job done since the computer will
do the work at its earliest opportunity -
usually within the next few seconds. There
is no need for any other information, such
as the name of your supervisor, since the
computer really doesn't need to know that.

Please proceed to Frame 23.

FRAME 23

What you want it to do is the correct response.
You tell the computer what you want done by
typing simple messages called "statements."
Here is an example of a BASIC statement:

$$200 \quad LET \ D = M + Y + 3.5$$

A statement, therefore is a message to the
computer telling it

24   What you want it to do.

25   What your ID is.

26   What programming language you intend
     using.

FRAME 24

Yes, with a statement you tell a computer what you want it to do. A statement has three parts. They are:

1. line number

2. key word

3. body of the statement

Here's an example:

200   LET D = M + Y + 3.5

Examine the statement. What would you say is the line number?

27   200

28   3.5

FRAME 25

No, this is not the point in which you tell
the computer what your ID is. You gave the
computer your ID at an earlier time.

Please return to Frame 23 and make another
selection.

FRAME 26

No, this is not the place in which you tell
the computer what program language you intend
to use. You gave the computer this information
in response to an earlier question.

Please go back and read Frame 23 again carefully, then make another selection.

FRAME 27

The correct response is 200. This number
identifies the statement. It's like giving
a statement a name except that the name must
always be a number.

In the same statement

200   LET D = M + Y + 3.5

What would you say is the key word?

29   LET

30   D

FRAME 28

No, your response is not correct. A statement has three parts. They are line number, key word, and body of the statement. We can eliminate the word LET as the answer to this frame, since LET isn't a number. Your decision now has to be between 3.5 and 200. The number 3.5 is not correct, since it appears to be a member of the equation $D = M + Y + 3.5$. This leaves only 200, which is correct. A line number is a number which appears furthest to the left in a statement.

Please continue with Frame 27.

FRAME 29

The key word is LET.

In the same statement, what would you say is the body of the statement?

31   LET

32   D = M + Y + 3.5

33   LET D = M + Y + 3.5

FRAME 30

The key word is not D because D is not a
word. The word LET is the correct choice.
The key word immediately follows the line
number.

Please continue with Frame 29.

FRAME 31

We've just agreed that LET is a key word. It cannot be the body of the statement at the same time. So, the body must be either D = M + Y + 3.5 or LET D = M + Y + 3.5. The latter choice can't be right, because it includes the key word LET. This leaves only D = M + Y + 3.5.

Please go now to Frame 32.

FRAME 32

The body is D = M + Y + 3.5.

This has to be the body of the statement, because the line number is easily identified as 200 and the key word is easily identified as LET. What remains has to be the body of the statement. You'll recall that every BASIC statement consists of three parts. From the choices below, select the element which is <u>not</u> a part of a BASIC statement:

34   Key word.

35   Your personal identification code (ID)

FRAME 33

No, LET D = M + Y + 3.5 is not the body of
the statement, since it includes the key word
LET.   The three parts of a statement are
entirely separate parts, (line number, key
word, and body of the statement).

Please go back to Frame 29 and make another
selection.

FRAME 34

Your answer is not correct. Please reread
Frame 28 carefully. The key word is definitely given as a part of a statement. By a
process of elimination, the identification
code must be the item which is not a part of
a BASIC statement.

Please go to Frame 35.

FRAME 35

The correct response is your personal identification code (ID). In telling the computer
what to do, you usually type not just one
BASIC statement, but a series. Here is a
sample:

```
100   LET W = 46
110   LET X = 94
120   LET Y = W + X
130   PRINT Y
140   END
```

These statements constitute "a program". A
program is a series of statements that tell
the computer what to do in order to solve a
given problem. How many statements would you
expect to find in a program?

36   Five.

37   There is no set number. It depends upon
     the problem being solved.

FRAME 36

Frame 35 states that a program usually consists of a series of statements. It doesn't
give any definite number, therefore, an
answer like "five" is incorrect. Five statements in a program are usually too few to accomplish much. A program may have 20, 30, 40,
or even more statements. If a problem is
complex, a program may have hundreds of statements.

Please go to Frame 37.

FRAME 37

There is no set number of statements in a
program. It depends upon the problem being
solved.

Programs may consist of only a few statements.
But on the other hand, they may contain over
a thousand. Do you remember what a program
is?

38   A series of statements telling the
     computer how to solve a particular
     problem.

39   An instruction which has three parts:
     line number, key word, and body.

40   A log-on procedure.

FRAME 38

Your response is correct. A program is a
series of statements which tell the computer
how to solve a given problem.

When you wish to type a statement, you first
type the line number, then you type the key
word, and finally you type the body of the
statement. Having typed these three elements,
you hit the keyboard key labeled RETURN.

When you hit this key, the computer accepts
the statement you typed. Up until this time
you may change your statement before hitting
RETURN, therefore, be sure that

41 You've given the computer your correct
   personal identification code (ID).

42 You've typed the statement you intended
   to type.

FRAME 39

An instruction is only part of a program. A program is a set of instructions which tell the computer what to do in order to solve a problem. An instruction tells the computer what to do to accomplish a certain objective in solving the entire problem. Your answer is therefore incorrect.

Please go back to Frame 38.

FRAME 40

No, the log-on procedure is not a program.
This is actually the sequence of questions
and responses which are made between you and
the computer when you first sign on.

A program is a series of instructions which
tell the computer what to do in order to
solve some given problem.

Please return to Frame 37. Read it again,
then make the correct response.

FRAME 41

Surely you don't mean to give this response.
The computer will not permit you to get this
far if at the very beginning you did not give
a valid identification code (ID). The correct
response is that you've typed the statement
you intended to type.

Don't be concerned about having inadvertently
returned the carriage. There are ways to
make corrections as you will see presently.

Please go on to Frame 42.

FRAME 42

The correct response is you've typed the statement you intended to type.

In programs the line numbers you type at the beginning of every BASIC statement must be in increasing sequence. The smallest you may use is 1, the largest, 99999. Suppose you write this BASIC statement:

        200   LET D = 2 - 9

Which of these line numbers may not be used for the next statement of a program?

43   350

44   105

FRAME 43

No, statement numbers must be in increasing
sequence. A statement having a line number
such as 201 or 350 may certainly be used as
the next statement of a program. After you
have typed statement 200, the next statement
which logically follows in your program must
be larger than 200. The only statement given
among those to choose from which is not acceptable in the current example is 105.

Please go to Frame 44.

FRAME 44

The correct choice is 105.

BASIC statements have key words immediately
following their line numbers. In this book
we will explain the key words LET, READ,
PRINT, IF, GO TO, DATA, INPUT, REM, DIM, FOR,
NEXT, RESTORE, ON, and END. With only 14 key
words, BASIC statements can be written to
solve amazingly complex problems.

Which of these next words is not a BASIC key
word?

45   DATA

46   DO

FRAME 45

Sorry, your answer is not correct. You should double check your response. A quick look at the 14 key words shown in Frame 44 indicates that the correct reply to the question is DO. The word DO is not a BASIC key word; the word DATA is definitely a key word.

Please advance to Frame 46.

FRAME 46

The correct response is DO. This word is
not a BASIC key word. Here is a complete
BASIC program. Please study, then answer
the question in this frame.

```
150   LET P = 21.7
190   LET Q = 46.8
220   LET V = P + Q
230   PRINT P,Q,V
240   END
```

How many BASIC statements are there in the
program?

47   240

48   5

FRAME 47

You probably don't clearly understand what a
BASIC statement is. A BASIC statement is an
instruction telling the computer what you
want done. A complete BASIC program is com-
posed of a set of statements. The correct
answer is 5.

At this point you should go back to Frame 23
to review what was said about BASIC statements.

FRAME 48
_____

Yes, you're right.   There are 5 statements
in the program.   How many <u>different</u> key
words are used in the program shown in
Frame 46.

49   5

50   8

51   3

FRAME 49

You said there are five key words in the
program shown in Frame 46. Did you look the
program over carefully? There are five
statements, but three of them begin with LET.

Please go back to Frame 48 and give another
response.

FRAME 50

How did you get eight as the correct response?
At this point you should review what BASIC
statements are. Please go back to Frame 23.

FRAME 51

Yes, there are three key words in the program.
They are LET, PRINT, and END.

What do you suppose the "+" symbol means in
line 220 of the program in Frame 46?

52   Divide

53   Add

FRAME 52

The symbol "+" means exactly what it does in
mathematics, add. In BASIC "+" means add;
"-" means subtract; "/" means divide; "*"
means multiply and "↟" means raise to a
power. We'll learn more about these arithmetic symbols later.

Please proceed to Frame 53.

FRAME 53

Yes "+" does mean add. Other symbols used
in BASIC are "-", "/", "*" and "↑". We'll
learn about these later.

What does the program in Frame 46 do?

54   Computes the sum of 21.7 and 46.8,
      then prints it.

55   Computes the product of 21.7 and 46.8,
      then prints it.

FRAME 54

Correct. The program computes the sum of
21.7 and 46.8, then prints it.

When you have typed in a complete program
and want to have the computer run it, type
the single word RUN. The computer will then
give the answer requested. Study this next
program:

```
100   LET W = 6.5
110   LET X = W * W
120   PRINT W,X
130   END
RUN
 6.5            42.25
```

Has the user typed 6.5 and 42.25 or has the
computer typed those numbers? Or, is another
answer more applicable?

56   The user has.

57   The computer has.

58   Neither.

FRAME 55

We admit we're asking you to make a guess
here. If you gave an incorrect answer don't
feel too badly. The program first stores
the value 21.7 in a place called P; then it
stores the value 46.8 in another place called
Q; next the program computes the sum of P and
Q, placing the result in V. Finally, the
program prints the values of P, Q, and V.

Please proceed to Frame 54.

FRAME 56

Again we're asking you to do some guessing.
You may not have known or correctly guessed
that "*" means multiply. The program first
stored the value 6.5 in W. Then it multiplied W times W (6.5 times 6.5), and stored
the result in X. Finally, the program
printed both W and X.

Therefore, the computer typed 6.5 and 42.25.
It wouldn't make much sense to have the programmer type these numbers would it?

Please go back to Frame 54 and study the program to satisfy yourself that what we said
above is true. Then select another response.

FRAME 57

Yes, the only possible answer is that the
computer has.

When you type RUN, the computer gives answers
that it calculates. Now if you want to save
the program for use at a later date, type
SAVE.

Examine this printout:

```
100   LET W = 6.5
110   LET X = W * W
120   PRINT W, X
130   END
RUN
 6.5            42.25
SAVE
READY
```

What is the name under which you saved this
program?

59   READY

60   There is not enough information given
     to tell.

FRAME 58

Did you really intend to give this answer or
were you joking? If the computer didn't type
the numbers and the programmer didn't, then
who did? If you were serious in your answer,
please return to Frame 54 and give another
response. If you were just joking, why not
take a break, then resume with Frame 57.

FRAME 59

No, this is not the correct response. You
may have selected this response through a
process of elimination since the second
choice doesn't appear to be correct. Actually, not enough information has been given to
enable you to answer the question because the
program was named when you first entered the
system. In response to NEW OR OLD, you replied NEW and gave the program a name.

To refresh your memory about how the name
actually was given, reread Frame 14. Then
proceed to Frame 60.

FRAME 60

The correct response is that "not enough
information has been given enabling you to
answer the question." Your answer is correct.
The program's name was given during the log-
on sequence. When you type SAVE, the computer
remembers the name of your program from the
log-on sequence and saves it with that name.

There is no response required for this frame.
Please go directly to Frame 61.

FRAME 61

Study the program in Frame 57. What would
you say the asterisk means in line 110?

62   See footnote.

63   Multiply

FRAME 62

No, the asterisk has nothing to do with a footnote. It simply indicates that one value is to be multiplied by another. In the example, W is to be multiplied by W. In BASIC, the asterisk means multiply.

Please continue with Frame 63.

FRAME 63

The asterisk means multiply.

This program assigns the value 6.5 to W, multiplies W by W (6.5 by 6.5), and prints out both W and W times W. Observe that the commands RUN and SAVE must not be preceded by line numbers.

When a person has finished his work at the terminal, he may type BYE to become disconnected immediately. Example:

```
100    LET W = 6.5
110    LET X = W * W
120    PRINT W, X
130    END
RUN
 6.5                 42.25
SAVE
READY
BYE
```

The system disconnects at this point. No response required for this frame. Congratulations for having completed Section I.

SECTION II

LET STATEMENT

FRAME 64

In Section I you learned some of the elemen-
tary facts concerning conversational timesharing. You learned, for example, that to
use a distant computer you must first make
arrangements to obtain a personal identification code (ID). The ID code must be given
when the computer requests it. You also
learned that in response to SYSTEM, you
must type BASIC. Finally, when the computer
requests NEW or OLD you must give the appropriate response, along with the program's
name.

You learned that to build a computer program
you must type a series of:

65   Error messages.

66   Equations.

67   Statements

FRAME 65

No, you are not the one who types the error
messages. The computer will do so if you
don't follow the rules precisely. (We'll
explain more about error messages later.)

You should recall that you must type a series
of statements forming a program. If your
understanding of statements and programs is
a little weak, why not begin again from the
beginning.

Please go to Frame 67.

FRAME 66

It's understandable that you would reply
equations, since so many people who use
BASIC are primarily interested in running
programs that work with equations. Actually,
the correct answer is statements. A statement such as

$$\text{LET } X = P + Q + R$$

appears to have an equation in it. Actually
it doesn't. This statement tells the computer to compute P plus Q plus R and to assign the result to X.

Please go to Frame 67.

FRAME 67

The correct response is statements.

At the conclusion of every statement, you must depress the RETURN key. Before you depress the RETURN key you may correct mistakes by depressing the backwards arrow(←) key. Here's an example:

$$305 \quad LEM \leftarrow T \quad P = 6$$

The M was typed in error. The typing of the backwards arrow enables the user to replace M with T. When you type a backwards arrow, therefore, you cancel:

68   The previously typed character.

69   The entire statement.

FRAME 68

The previously typed character is the correct response.

Should you wish to cancel more than one character, you may type two or more backwards arrows. Example:

      510   PRENT ← ← ←INT B,C

The characters INT replace

70   ENT

71   INT

72   T only

FRAME 69

No, the backwards arrow does not cancel the
entire statement. The backwards arrow merely
cancels the last character typed. There are
ways to cancel entire statements, even entire
programs, but we'll have to wait a while before learning how to accomplish these tasks.

Please go on to Frame 68.

70

FRAME 70

Yes, the correct response is ENT.

After a statement has been typed and the
RETURN key depressed, it is too late to
make corrections using the backwards arrow.
If you need to make corrections to a statement, you must retype the statement. Here's
an example:

```
100   LET D = 5
110   LET E = 66
120   LET F = D + E
130   PLINK D, E, F
130   PRINT D, E, F
110   LET E = 6
140   END
```

How many statements were corrected in this
program?

73   2

74   1

75   7

FRAME 71

The characters ENT will be replaced, not INT.
If you'll look at the statement being typed,
you'll see that it begins with PRENT (which
is wrong). Therefore, your response is incorrect.

Please return to Frame 68 and make another
selection.

FRAME 72

No, there will be three characters replaced,
not just one. That's the reason there are
three arrows following the characters PRENT,
one for each character replaced. If you
wanted to replace only T, then there would
be one backwards arrow following the letter
T.

Please return to Frame 68 and make another
selection.

FRAME 73

There were two statements corrected. The one
at line 110 and at line 130. Note that the
statement at line 130 was corrected immediately
after it was typed. The mistake at line 110
was noticed later, but was corrected.

How many statements does this program contain?

76   2

77   5

78   7

FRAME 74

No, the answer is not 1. You probably
didn't study the program carefully. Go
back to Frame 70 and look at lines 130 and
110. The statement at line 130 was incorrectly entered, then immediately corrected
(PRINT in place of PLINK). Also the statement at line 110 was incorrectly entered,
but the correction (LET in place of LED) did
not take place until later in the program.
Corrections may be made at any time. When
a line is retyped, the previous line having
the same number is replaced.

Please go to Frame 73.

FRAME 75

No, your response appears to be a guess.
It's true that there are 7 typed statements
in the example, but this fact has nothing to
do with the question. The question was how
many statements were corrected.

If your response was an accident, please
return to Frame 70 and make another selection.
If your response was your best answer to the
question, please return to Frame 64 and begin
this section again.

FRAME 76

No, the program contains many more than two
statements. Study the program. There are
statements at lines 100, 110, 120, 130, and
140. Five statements altogether.

You seem to be having some trouble understanding the questions in this section.
Review Section I before going on to Frame 77.

FRAME 77

The correct response is 5.

In the computer's memory the program contains
five statements. They are:

```
100   LET D = 5
110   LET E = 6
120   LET F = D + E
130   PRINT D, E, F
140   END
```

Each of these statements includes a key word.
The key word appearing in most statements is:

79   LET

80   RUN

FRAME 78

It's understandable that you would respond 7
to this question, since there were 7 typed
lines in the example. Don't overlook the
fact, though, that two lines replaced two
incorrect statements. Therefore, actually,
there are 5 statements in the program.

Please go on to Frame 77.

FRAME 79

The key word appearing most often is LET.
This is the first key word we will discuss
thoroughly.

Statements in which the key word LET appears
are called "assignment" statements. This
term is used because an assignment statement
gives (assigns) to some name a definite
value or a computation result.

Example:

$$800 \quad LET \ W = 17.2$$

In this statement the value assigned to W is

81   Unknown

82   17.2

83   800

FRAME 80

No, RUN should not have been given as the
response to this question. The correct
response is LET. You appear to be guessing.
Why not return to Section I for a review
before advancing to Frame 79.

FRAME 81

The value is indeed known. It is 17.2.
Your answer is incorrect. Please return to
Frame 79 and reread carefully. Then make
another response.

FRAME 82

Yes, the value 17.2 is assigned to 120.

In an assignment statement, the word LET is always followed by an equals sign (=). To the right of an equals sign we may see either a literal number such as 17.2, a name such as F, or a calculation such as (P*Q)/2.

What may appear to the right of an equals sign?

84 A literal number or a name.

85 A literal number, a name, or a calculation.

FRAME 83

No, the number 800 is not the value that is
being assigned to W. Actually the value is
17.2. You are confusing the line number of
the statement (800) with the value to be
assigned to W. Please return to Frame 79
and read it carefully. Then, make another
selection.

FRAME 84

No, you didn't read the frame carefully.
To the right of the equals sign may be one
of three possible items: a value such as
17.2 or -8.1; a name such as F or H; or a
calculation to be made such as (P*Q)/2 or
(W+F) * (G-H).

The correct response would have directed
you to Frame 85. Please go there now.

FRAME 85

The correct response is a literal (actual)
number, a name, or a calculation.

Study this series of assignment statements:

```
100   LET P = 40
110   LET Q = 90
120   LET R = P + Q
130   LET Q = 6
140   LET S = P + Q
150   LET T = P
```

What values has the program assigned to P,
Q, R, S and T?

86   40, 6, 130, 130, and 40

87   40, 6, 130, 46, and 40

FRAME 86

No, you slipped up somewhere. Please follow what happened.

First the program assigned 40 to P. Now P holds the value 40.

Then the program assigned 90 to Q. Now Q holds the value 90.

Then the program assigned P + Q (40 + 90) to R. Now R holds 130.

Then the program assigned 6 to Q. This changed Q's value from 90 to 6. The change to Q did not change the values previously assigned to P and R.

Then the program assigned P + Q (40 + 6) to S. Now S holds 46.

Finally, the program assigned P's value (40) to T. Now T holds the value 40.

The last values assigned to P, Q, R, S, and T are therefore, 40, 6, 130, 46, and 40.

Please go back to Frame 85 and convince yourself that this is true. Then continue with Frame 87.

FRAME 87

The correct values are 40, 6, 130, 46, and 40.

The program assigns values in the same sequence in which the assignment statements are presented. First the program assigns 40 to P. Then the program assigns 90 to Q. Then the program assigns the result of the calculation P + Q. to R. At the time the calculation is made, the value of P is 40 and the value of Q is 90. Therefore, the value assigned to R is 130. The next assignment statement is

130   LET Q = 6

At this point, the value assigned to Q is:

88   6

89   90

FRAME 88

The correct response is 6.

The current value assigned to Q replaces the value of Q at line 110. From this point on whenever Q is used for any purpose, Q will have the value 6. The fact that Q now holds 6, whereas it once held 40, does not cause the program to recalculate R which was calculated at line 120. R retains its old value of 130.

The next assignment statement is:

$$140 \quad LET \ S = P + Q$$

The value that the program assigns to S is:

90   46

91   6

FRAME 89

No, we thought you had it straight. The old
value of Q was 90. The new value assigned to
Q is 6. The value 130 is what was earlier
assigned to R. It's important to observe
that when a new value is given to Q, calculations made earlier using Q are not changed.
When Q's value is changed to 6, R's value
remains at 130.

Please return to Frame 85 and resume studying
from that point.

FRAME 90

Good!

The program assigns 46 to S because the value currently stored in P and Q are 40 and 6, respectively.

Finally, the program assigns the value of P to T. Since the current value of P is 40, the program assigns 40 to T.

In an assignment statement, the actual value or calculation shown on the right hand side of the equals sign is assigned to the name shown on the left hand side of the equals sign.

Would you say that an assignment statement always uses the key word LET and an equals sign?

92   Yes.

93   No.

94   Sometimes the equals sign may be
     omitted.

FRAME 91

No, something has gone wrong. Your response is not correct. The value assigned to S is the sum of the values last assigned to P and Q. The value last assigned to P was 40. The value last assigned to Q was 6. Therefore, the sum of P and Q is 46. This is the value assigned to R.

Please return to Frame 85 and resume study at that point.

FRAME 92

The answer is Yes.

An assignment statement often gives, on the right hand side of the equals sign, a calculation to be performed.
Example:

600   LET F = (A + B) / (A - B)

This statement requires A to be added to B, for B to be subtracted from A, and for the first result to be divided by the second result.   In this statement + means add, - means subtract, and / means divide.   What would you say the (*) does in this next assignment statement?

700   LET G = (A + B) * C

95   Multiplication of A + B by C.

96   Multiplication of B by C.

97   Division by zero.

FRAME 93

Although the word LET may be omitted on some systems, you really should have answered Yes, because the text did not mention the exception given above.

Please reread Frame 90 carefully. Then give another response.

FRAME 94

No, the equal sign may never be omitted.
Where did you get that idea? Please reread
Frame 90 carefully and give another response.

FRAME 95

The statement causes the multiplication of
A + B by C. An assignment statement may be
used to instruct the computer to make a calculation and to assign the result of that
calculation to some name. Suppose you want
the computer to make this calculation:

$$\frac{99.6}{3.5} + \frac{8.7}{5.6 - 2.2}$$

How would you write the BASIC statement?

98   500   LET F = (99.6/3.5) + 8.7/5.6 - 2.2

99   500   LET F = 99.6/3.5 + 8.7/(5.6 - 2.2)

FRAME 96

No, your answer is not right. Why did you
ignore A? Actually, A is added to B, then
the quantity is divided by C. Please return
to Frame 92 and make a better selection.

FRAME 97

Why do you give this response? The frame
gives no hint that this might be a correct
answer. Please return to Frame 92, reread
it, then give a better response.

FRAME 98

You gave an incorrect answer, but perhaps
it wasn't your fault. We didn't cover how
to perform calculations that are more complex than the ones covered earlier.

Parentheses are used to group quantities.
The rules for grouping closely match the
rules followed in ordinary mathematics.
The quantity which must be grouped is 5.6 -
2.2. Unless you had parentheses around
this quantity, your statement would be
wrong.

The correct frame to go to was 99. Please
go there now.

FRAME 99

The correct statement is

  500 LET F = 99.6/3.5 + 8.7/(5.6 - 2.2).

The quantity 5.6 - 2.2 must be enclosed in parentheses, otherwise the computer will think that you want it to compute:

$$\frac{99.6}{3.5} + \frac{8.7}{5.6} - 2.2$$

There is a natural order that the computer uses when doing arithmetic operations. <u>When parentheses don't indicate otherwise</u>, the computer does <u>multiplications</u> and <u>divisions</u> before doing <u>additions and subtractions.</u>

In this next statement, what would you say the computer does first?

        350 LET G = X + Y - Z/D

100 Z is subtracted from Y.

101 Z is divided by D.

FRAME 100

No, the frame clearly states that multiplications and divisions are done before additions and subtractions. There is only one calculation in the statement which is not an addition or subtraction.

Please return to Frame 99 and see if you can find that calculation.

FRAME 101

Exactly right! Z is divided by D.

In Section III we will cover math calculations
in more detail. For now, let's review the
fact that + means add, - means subtract, *
means multiply, and / means divide.

Suppose you need to compute: *5TH POWER*

$$7.4^5 \leftarrow$$

you could instruct the computer to do this:

   9050   LET J = 7.4 * 7.4 * 7.4 * 7.4 * 7.4

An easier way to accomplish the same objective
is:

        9050   LET J = 7.4 ↑ 5

The upwards pointing arrow permits:

102   An error to be corrected.

103   A value to be multiplied by another.

104   A value to be raised to a power.

FRAME 102

No, the upwards arrow has nothing to do with errors. You may have confused this arrow with the left pointing arrow (←) which does permit certain error corrections. Actually, the upward arrow permits values to be raised to powers. The statement:

9050   LET J = 7.4 ↑ 5

causes the calculation

7.4 x 7.4 x 7.4 x 7.4 x 7.4

Please proceed to Frame 104.

FRAME 103

You're partially right. The upward arrow causes values to be multiplied as often as needed to obtain the desired result.

Thus,

$$9050 \quad \text{LET } J = 7.4 \uparrow 5$$

raises J to the 5 power. This means that the calculation:

$$7.4 \times 7.4 \times 7.4 \times 7.4 \times 7.4$$

takes place.

Please proceed to Frame 104.

FRAME 104

The answer is "a value to be raised to a power." Suppose you need this calculation:

$$2.1^3 + 8.3^{2.4}$$

How would you write it?

105   90   LET D = 2.1 ↑ 3 + 8.3 ↑ 2.4

106   93   LET D = 2.1 * 3 + 8.3 * 2.4

FRAME 105

Yes, the correct response is:

$$90 \quad \text{LET } D = 2.1 \uparrow 3 + 8.3 \uparrow 2.4.$$

Let's leave math now until Section III and begin discussing BASIC data names. In previous frames we've used names like A, B, X, Y in assignment statements. Do you suppose any single letter of the alphabet could be used as a data name?

107   Yes.

108   No.

109   Probably not.

FRAME 106

Your way of causing the required calculation to take place is imaginative, but not correct. Remember, powers are handled with the upwards pointing arrow. Thus 2.1^3 is $2.1 \uparrow 3$ and $8.3^{2.4}$ is $8.3 \uparrow 2.4$

Please return to Frame 104 and make a better selection.

FRAME 107

Yes, a single letter of the alphabet can be used as a data name.

In a LET statement, you may write such instructions as:

```
10   LET A = 6
20   LET B = 9
30   LET G = A + B
```

Any letter from A through Z may follow the key word LET in an assignment statement. The computer sets aside a memory cell with the name you've given and holds the assigned value for the duration of the program or until a subsequent statement, which you give, changes it. How would you change the value which was assigned to G in line 30 above?

110   95   LET G = A * B

111   95   LET G ◄◄◄A * B

FRAME 108

Actually the answer should be Yes. Any
single letter of the alphabet can be used as
a name and can hold a value. We asked you
to make a guess. Sorry, you didn't guess
correctly.

Please continue with Frame 107.

FRAME 109

Your answer indicates you might suspect a
trap. Actually, the answer is Yes. Any
single letter of the alphabet may be used as
the name to which a value may be assigned.

Please continue with Frame 107.

FRAME 110

The correct way to change G's value is with

95   LET G = A * B

As you've already seen, when you assign another value to some name later in a pro-gram, the new value replaces the old one.

Memory cell names are called variable names. Thus in the statement

95   LET G = A * B

The names A, B and G are called variable names. The reason this term applies is because <u>any</u> values may be assigned to those names during the execution of a program.

A variable name may also consist of a single letter followed by a single digit. Examples include F3, G7, X5, and P0.

Which statement below would you say is wrong?

112   100   LET G3 = 17

113   110   LET 3L = -9.6

114   120   LET F8 = -2.1

FRAME 111

No, your way of changing the value assigned
earlier to a memory cell is too elaborate.
Nor does it work.

You might try backwards arrows (◄—), but that
will not work after you have depressed the
RETURN key.

The simplest method is to give another assignment statement. When you type

                95   LET G = A * B

You replace the value which was given to G
at line 30.

Please proceed to Frame 110.

FRAME 112

No, the statement is correct. The variable
name G3 is legal, because variable names may
consist of a single letter followed by a
single digit.

Please return to Frame 110 and make a better
selection.

FRAME 113

Fine!   The variable name 3L is wrong.

Variable name G3 is acceptable, because a variable name may consist of a single alphabetic character followed by a single digit. F8 is OK for the same reason.

Variable name 3L is wrong because a variable name may not consist of a single digit followed by a single letter.

Would you say that the following statement is correct?

          250   LET TOM = 19.76

115   Yes.

116   No.

117   It might be, sometimes.

FRAME 114

No, your response is not correct. The statement at line 120 is OK. The variable name F8 is correct because a name may consist of a single alphabetic character followed by a single digit.

Please return to Frame 110 and make a better selection.

FRAME 115

No, we have to insist that in BASIC a variable
name may only consist of a single letter of the
alphabet or a single letter of the alphabet
followed by a single digit. TOM is not a valid
name.

Please return to Frame 113 and make a better
selection.

FRAME 116

No is the correct response. The variable
name TOM is wrong because a BASIC variable
name may not have more than two characters,
which must consist of a single letter of the
alphabet followed by a single digit.

Here is a correct assignment statement that
at first glance might look strange.

$$2000 \quad LET \ R = R + 5$$

How can the variable name R appear on both
sides of the equals sign?

118   It can't. The statement is wrong.

119   The old value of R is used to
      compute a new value of R.

120   This must be new math.

FRAME 117

No, since TOM is never a variable name, the statement can never be correct. Unless you're jesting, you don't seem to understand how assignment statements work. Please repeat the frames of this section beginning at Frame 64.

If you were just kidding, go on to Frame 116.

FRAME 118

Actually, the statement is correct.

Please review Frame 116 and see if you can
select a better response.

FRAME 119

Yes, the old value of R is used to compute a
new value of R.

In the statement

        2000   LET R = R + 5

whatever value R holds is added to 5. Then
the result of the calculation is assigned
back to R. R is thus "updated" and the old
value of R disappears. The same memory cell
is used to store both Rs.

Suppose the old value of R was 18. What is
the new value of R?

121 18[5]

122 23

FRAME 120

No, new math has nothing to do with this.
The statement has a very simple and straight
forward meaning.

Please go back to Frame 116 to see if you
can make a better selection.

FRAME 121

No, you didn't read the frame closely enough.
To compute a new value for R, you must add 5
to the old value. Since R's old value was 18,
the new value has to be 23.

Please reread Frame 119 then go on to Frame 122.

FRAME 122

The correct response is 23.

In an assignment statement having the same
variable name on both sides of the equals
sign, the old value disappears when the new
value is computed. Obviously, a program
should use this type of assignment statement only when it is not important to keep
the old value. In counting, a program may
use a statement like

$$605 \quad LET \ C = C + 1$$

in which 1 is added to the counting variable.
In this example the name chosen as the counting variable is C.

We'll discuss counters again when we cover
loops in Section IV. No response is required
for this frame. Congratulations for having
successfully completed Section II.

SECTION III

ARITHMETIC

FRAME 123

In previous frames you learned that assignment statements may be used to instruct the computer to make calculations then store the results at named memory locations.

You also learned that five types of arithmetic operations may be employed: +, -, *, /, and ⬆. Parentheses should be used extensively in order to make the meanings of certain expressions (calculations) clear.

When parentheses are not used in an expression, the computer does exponentiations (raising to powers) before other operations. What does it do before addition and subtractions?

124 Multiplications and divisions.

125 Nothing. The computer goes directly to the additions and subtractions.

FRAME 124

Yes, multiplications and divisions.

In scanning an expression from left to right the program zeroes in on parentheses first, then tries to find parentheses inside of parentheses. Having taken this step, the computer begins making calculations. Study this statement:

850   LET M = P + R + (D↑3 + (S * T / U↑2) + L)

What calculation will the computer perform first?

126   D ↑ 3

127   U ↑ 2

128   P + R

FRAME 125

Sorry, your answer is not correct. When parentheses are not used, the computer raises to
powers first (exponentiates), next multiplications and divisions in whatever order from
left to right they occur in the expression,
and finally the computer adds and subtracts.

Based upon this additional explanatory information, can you now select a better response
from Frame 123.

FRAME 126

You're right in thinking that an exponentiation will be performed, but you selected
the wrong one. Observe that U↑2 is inside
an innermost set of parentheses. The computer finds innermost parentheses first,
then looks for exponentiations there.

Please proceed directly to Frame 127.

FRAME 127

U↑2 is the correct answer.

You'll observe that U↑2 is shown as a calculation within the innermost of two sets of
parentheses in the expression. Since exponentiations are computed before anything else,
the U↑2 term is evaluated first.

The program then multiplies S by T and divides
the result of this calculation by the result
of the U↑2 calculation.

Which calculation does the computer perform
next?

129 D↑3

130 It is impossible to tell from the
     expression.

FRAME 128

No, P + R is not correct, the computer looks for innermost parentheses first. Please return to Frame 124 and find a set of parentheses inside another set of parentheses. Then decide which operation will be performed first and give another answer.

FRAME 129

Good! The computer evaluates D↑3.

The computer has now effectively changed the
original statement to this one:

    850   LET M = P + R + (D↑3 + X + L)

X was not in the original expression, but it
was created by the computer when the calculations representing (S * T / U↑2) were made.
The computer makes these calculations, then
assigns the result to a variable name which
is unknown to the user (it might not actually
be X). Don't worry that the computer will
select a name which you have already selected for your program. It won't.

D↑3 is an exponentiation in the set of remaining parentheses. D↑3 has priority over
additions, so the program computes D↑3 next.
There is no response required for this frame.

Please go to Frame 131.

FRAME 130

Your answer indicates that you really don't
understand what we have discussed so far.
Please return to Frame 123 and carefully
study the material leading to Frame 127.

FRAME 131

The program adds the result of D↑3 to X and
to L. This result is then assigned to another
name known only to the computer. By this time
the expression has been reduced to

$$850 \quad \text{LET } M = P + R + Y$$

We're assuming the computer assigns the name
Y to the result of (D↑3 + X + L). The rest
of the evaluation is simple. The computer

132   Adds P, R and Y and assigns the result
      to M.

133   Adds R and P, but saves Y for a later
      calculation.

FRAME 132

The computer adds P, R and Y and assigns
the result to M.

You may sometimes wonder whether a set of
parentheses is needed in an expression.
For example, suppose you want to have the
computer make this calculation:

$$\frac{\dfrac{2.6}{9.4}}{6.8}$$

Could you enter the instruction this way?

60   LET F = 2.6 / 9.4 / 6.8

134   Yes.

135   No.

136   Yes, but half the time you'll get
the wrong answer.

FRAME 133

No, nothing in this text has suggested anything as exotic as your reply would happen.

The statement

       850   LET M = P + R + Y

calls for a very straight forward sequence
of operations. The computer adds the values
last assigned to P, R, and Y, then assigns
the result to M.

Please return to Frame 123 and study all the
frames again leading to Frame 131.

FRAME 134

The answer is yes.

The computer divides 2.6 by 9.4, then divides the result by 6.8. This is exactly what you want. If you had not been sure what the computer would do with the statement you could have entered:

        60   LET F = (2.6 / 9.4) / 6.8

The result would have been the same and these extra parentheses would have caused no extra trouble or expense.

Could you solve the same problem by typing the statement this way?

        60   LET F = 2.6 / (9.4 / 6.8)

137   Yes

138   No

139   Is this not the same question as in Frame 132?

FRAME 135

No is not a correct response.

When you give a BASIC statement representing

$$\frac{\frac{2.6}{9.4}}{6.8}$$

you could give

    60   LET F = (2.6 / 9.4) / 6.8

but this expression will give the same result as

    60   LET F = 2.6 / 9.4 / 6.8

The reason is that 2.6 will be divided by 9.4 and the result will be divided by 6.8.

Your answer should have been Yes.

Please proceed to Frame 134.

FRAME 136

No, a computer program doesn't work the way
you suspect. A BASIC statement is an order
to the computer to perform certain operations.
The computer will work out a statement the
same way every time executed.

Please return to Frame 132 and select a
better response.

FRAME 137

No, this time the computer will compute 9.4 /
6.8 and divide 2.6 by that result. You actually would be computing

$$\frac{\dfrac{2.6}{9.4}}{6.8}$$

This computation is far different from

$$\frac{2.6}{\dfrac{9.4}{6.8}}$$

Please return to Frame 132 and work your way
forward again to Frame 134.

FRAME 138

Your answer (No) is correct.

The program will first divide 9.4 by 6.8, then divide 2.6 by the result just obtained. Whenever you are not sure whether a set of parentheses should be employed or not, include them. The parentheses will help tell the computer exactly what you want done. The computer will have no choice but to follow your orders. When you do include parentheses, double check your statement to make sure you've correctly instructed the computer.

Now let's discuss functions. A function is a series of BASIC statements which the BASIC system offers to you free for the asking. An example is:

        9050 LET J = SQR (2.3)

Can you correctly guess what the computer will give you?

140   The square root of 2.3.

141   The square root of J.

142   The contents of the subquotient register.

FRAME 139

No, this is not the same question as in Frame
132. You've missed the point we're trying to
make about when parentheses are not needed in
an expression and when they are.

Please return to Frame 132 and work your way
forward again to Frame 134. Study the material
carefully.

FRAME 140

Yes, the program computes the square root of 2.3.

The SQR function, therefore, is a function which you may call for whenever you need a square root. You might want the square root of 2.3 or of N or of (P + L) / D. Here is the way you could ask for these three square roots:

```
100   LET B = SQR (2.3)
110   LET C = SQR (N)
120   LET F = SQR ( (P + L) / D)
```

These statements are taken out of context. You must assume that the variables N, P, L, and D were assigned actual values earlier in the program.

If you want to employ the built-in sine function, which of these statements would you write:

143   400   LET B = SQR (M)

144   400   LET B = SIN (M)

FRAME 141

It's true we asked for a guess, but you should
realize that your answer is not correct. A
variable name at the left hand side of the
equals sign always receives the result of a
calculation. The function could not, therefore, compute the square root of J.

Study Frame 138 again to see if you can make
a better choice.

FRAME 142

No, your answer is not at all consistent with what has been discussed so far. You should not continue with this section. We suggest you return to Frame 123 and begin again from that point.

FRAME 143

Admittedly we asked you to guess again, but
why did you select this response instead of
the more obvious one

$$400 \quad LET \ B = SIN(M)$$

Notice that sine and SIN are very close to
each other in spelling. You already know
that SQR means square root.

Please proceed to Frame 144.

FRAME 144

The correct statement is

400   LET B = SIN (M)

The SIN function is built into the BASIC language. This function enables you to obtain the sine of an angle when you give the angle in radian measure. You place the value of the angle within parentheses. The information you place in parentheses is called the argument of the function.

Do you agree that the argument of the SIN function, or any other function, may be a number such as 2.1, a name such as D, or an expression such as P * R?

145   Yes.

146   No.

FRAME 145

Yes, any function, be it SQR, SIN, COS, LOG, and others may have an actual number as its argument. Example:

        100   LET F = COS (1.3)

or a name,

        110   LET G = SQR (L)

or an expression,

     120   LET A = LOG (E - K * (S / T))

What would you say is the argument in the LOG function shown above?

147   S / T

148   E - K * (S / T)

149   There is no argument. The computer will
      obey the instruction.

FRAME 146

The correct response is Yes. For any function, such as: SQR; SIN; COS; and others,
the argument may be either an actual value
(2.1),

Example:

        300   LET M = SQR(2.1)

or a variable name (D),

        500   LET N = SIN(D)

or an expression ((E + F) / G),

      600   LET P = COS ((E + F) / G).

Please continue with Frame 145.

FRAME 147

No, there's more to the argument than S/T.
An argument of a function includes everything
within the outer parentheses given with all
functions. An argument may itself include
parentheses. Thus, in

        120   LET A = LOG (E - K * (S / T))

the outer parentheses enclose

              E - K * (S / T)

which is the argument of the function.

Please proceed to Frame 148.

FRAME 148

Yes, the argument is E - K * (S / T)

The argument of a function must be enclosed within a pair of parentheses. If the argument contains an expression, that expression may contain its own pair or pairs of parentheses.

The functions built into BASIC are: SQR; SIN; COS; TAN; LOG; EXP; RND; INT; and ABS.

As we've seen, SQR is used to obtain square roots, SIN to obtain sines of angles, and COS to obtain cosines of angles. What about TAN?

150   It is used to obtain tangents of angles.

151   It is used as a temporary array name.

FRAME 149

This is just a gag response. If you recog-
nized it as such, proceed to Frame 148, otherwise go back to Frame 144 and proceed forward
from that point.

FRAME 150

Yes, TAN is used to obtain tangents of angles. The clue is "tan" in the word tangent.

The INT function is used to obtain the largest whole number (integer) available in a given number. Thus in

750 LET X = INT (F)

the value assigned to X is 17, if X equals either 17.8 or 17.3.

What will the computer assign to Y in the next statement?

760 LET Y = INT (G + H)

(Assume that G holds the value 7.4 and H holds the value 7.7.)

152 15

153 14

FRAME 151

No, your answer is not correct. You don't seem to understand what we've been discussing about functions. Please return to Frame 138 and proceed from there.

FRAME 152

The correct answer is 15.

The program first obtains the value of the argument, then obtains the integer result. Since 7.4 plus 7.7 equals 15.1, the program assigns 15 to Y.

The ABS function assigns the absolute value of an expression to the appropriate variable name. In

        770   LET Z = ABS(L)

The program assigns 46.3 to Z, if L equals either 46.3 or -46.3. In either case, Z's value is a positive number.

What would you guess the LOG function does?

154   It computes the natural logarithm of the argument.

155   Log-on procedure provides an optional value.

FRAME 153

Your answer is not correct.

The computer first evaluates the G + H part of the expression. That is, the computer adds 7.4 and 7.7. The result is 15.1. Then it obtains the integer portion of that value. The largest integer in 15.1 is 15. Therefore, 15 is assigned to Y.

Please reread Frame 150 to satisfy yourself that the correct answer to the frame is indeed 15. Then proceed to Frame 152.

FRAME 154

Yes, LOG computes the natural logarithm of the given argument.

EXP is used to raise "e" to some given power. To mathematicians, the value of "e" is 2.718281828.... (The dots indicate that this is a never ending value.) Suppose you wish to raise "e" to the power 7.4. You could accomplish the task this way:

190   LET J = 2.71828↑7.4

or more simply

190   LET J = EXP (7.4)

RND is used to obtain random numbers. Example:

200   LET K = RND (X)

The number obtained lies between zero and one. (Zero is possible to attain, but the number will never actually be as large as one.) A further discussion of random numbers is beyond the scope of this text.

Congratulations for successfully completing Section III.

FRAME 155

You seem to be having a great deal of difficulty understanding functions and arguments. A function name always begins with something that suggests what the function does mathematically. Thus SIN suggests sine; COS suggests cosine; TAN suggests tangent; INT suggests integer; etc. The LOG function computes the natural logarithms of terms given within parentheses (arguments).

Please return to Frame 138 where the discussion of functions begins and proceed forward from that point.

SECTION IV

PRINT AND
IF STATEMENT

FRAME 156

A series of assignment statements will by
themselves never make a program. Somewhere
along the line a PRINT statement will have
to be given so that the outside world can
be informed about what the computer has
calculated. Study this program:

```
2000   LET D = (2.9 * 5.86) / 4.8
2010   PRINT D
2020   END
```

This program makes a calculation and assigns
the result to D. Then the program prints the
value that was just computed. Which of the
three statements in this program is the PRINT
statement?

157   Line 2000.

158   Line 2010.

FRAME 157

No, the statement at line 2000 is a LET statement. The first word of a statement tells the
kind of a statement it is. Observe that the
word PRINT appears at line 2010. This is the
PRINT statement.

Please proceed to Frame 158.

FRAME 158

Yes, the statement at line 2010 is the PRINT
statement.

In previous frames you learned that assignment
statements always included the key word LET.
By the same token, PRINT statements always
include the key word PRINT. You may place as
many PRINT statements in a program as you
need.

In a PRINT statement, the information concerning what you want the computer to print
is placed to the right of the key word PRINT.

Thus, if you want the program to print the
current value assigned to D, you would enter
the PRINT statement:

159   50 PRINT D

160   50 PRINT VALUE OF D

161   50 PRINT

FRAME 159

Yes, 50 PRINT D is the correct statement.

This statement shows that you want the computer to print the last value assigned to D. The value of D is then typed by the computer on the left hand side of the output paper.

The computer waits for your signal to execute a program. When you type RUN, the program is executed. Here's an example:

```
2000   LET D = - (2.9 * 5.86) / 4.8
2010   PRINT D
2020   END
RUN
-3.54042
```

What word above gives the signal that you want the program to be executed?

162   LET

163   RUN

FRAME 160

PRINT VALUE OF D is not correct. The form
of the PRINT statement is much simpler.
You enter the word PRINT and tell the computer what to PRINT.

Please return to Frame 158 and see if you
can make a better selection.

FRAME 161

No, the word PRINT by itself does not tell the computer which value you want printed. The correct procedure is to enter the word PRINT and give the name of the value desired.

Please return to Frame 158 and see if you can make a better selection.

FRAME 162

No, the word LET signals the beginning of a
LET statement.

The word RUN instructs the computer to execute
the program which has just been entered.

Please go to Frame 163.

FRAME 163

The correct response is RUN.

The word RUN is never preceded by a line
number, because it is a "system command."
System commands are never preceded by line
numbers. Other system commands you will
learn about are LIST, SAVE, UNSAVE, BYE, OLD,
and NEW. Each of these system commands accomplishes a specific task. What specific
task does RUN accomplish?

164 RUN tells the computer that you want
     the program you've entered saved.

165 RUN tells the computer that you want
     the program you've entered executed.

FRAME 164

No, your answer is not correct. The system
commands RUN, LIST, SAVE, etc. perform tasks
which the words themselves suggest. Thus,
RUN tells the computer to execute a program;
LIST tells the computer to list it; etc.

We'll cover system commands in detail as we
proceed in this text. The present question
concerns what RUN accomplishes. Please return to Frame 163 and make a better selection.

FRAME 165

Yes, RUN tells the computer that you want the
program you've entered executed.

The example program given above includes a
statement that we haven't said much about.
It's the END statement. Every program must
have an END statement, which must be the very
last one of your program. That is, it must
be the one which is preceded by the highest
line number.

In the example program, which is the very last
statement?

166　The END statement.

167　RUN.

168　The PRINT statement.

166

FRAME 166

The END statement is always the last statement of every program.

The END statement is the very last statement
of the example program. Observe that it has
the highest line number. The word RUN is not
a statement of your program. Only statements
with preceding line numbers are program statements. RUN is a system command.

Look at the example program again. In what
print position on the output paper did the
computer begin the answer?

169　Print position 1.

170　Print position 30.

FRAME 167

No, your response is not correct.

The word RUN, which follows the program, is not a portion of the program. RUN is actually a system command that tells the computer you want the program executed.

All statements in a program have line numbers. The statement which has the highest line number is END. It is, therefore, the very last statement.

Please return to Frame 165 and make another selection.

FRAME 168

No, your reply is not correct. The PRINT
statement does not have the highest line
number in the program. You missed that
important point. Please return to Frame 165
and reread it carefully, then make a better
selection.

FRAME 169

The computer prints the answer at print position 1.

The answer (-3.54042) begins at print position 1. Every line of the program begins in position 1. That is, lines 2000, 2010, and 2020 print beginning at print position 1. So does the word RUN. So does the answer. What is the print position of number 2 in the answer?

171   7

172   8

173   2

FRAME 170

No, study Frame 159 carefully. You'll see
that print position 30 is far to the right
of where the computer actually typed -3.54042.
The minus sign clearly prints in print position
1.

Observe that the left margin of the output
paper is assumed to be near where the 2s in
line numbers 2000, 2010, and 2020 are printed;
also where the R in the word RUN is shown.
The print position at those points is considered print position 1.

Please proceed to Frame 169.

FRAME 171

No, you have miscounted. Observe that the answer has eight characters (the minus sign and the decimal point actually do occupy print positions).

Please return to Frame 169 and make a better selection.

FRAME 172

Yes, the print position is 8.

The answer given by the computer is -3.54042. The print positions used to print the answer are:

Character Printed	Print Position
-	1
3	2
.	3
5	4
4	5
0	6
4	7
2	8

There are 72 print positions available on Teletype Model 33. This terminal is widely used in timesharing work, although several other types may also be used.

What is the maximum number of characters you may print on a single line using Teletype Model 33?

174   72

175   15

FRAME 173

No, you missed something. The character "3" is in print position 2. We're asking for the print position of the digit "2".

To get a fuller understanding of what is being discussed, please return to Frame 166 and proceed from that point.

FRAME 174

There are 72 print positions available.

Since 72 print positions are available, you may enter 72 characters on a single line. Imbedded blanks must be counted. Study this statement:

        2000 LET F=(4.4+8.94)/2.183

In what print position will the "3" be located?

176   3

177   27

178   26

FRAME 175

No, 15 characters per line would be entirely
too few. Many terminals have a capacity of
72 characters of information per line. Some
terminals permit up to 120 characters. The
best answer to the question is 72.

Please proceed directly to Frame 174.

FRAME 176

No, in print position 3, the third digit of
line number 2000 appears. You seem to have
misunderstood what we've been discussing
about print positions. Please go back to
Frame 172 and reread what has been said concerning print positions, then proceed.

FRAME 177

The print position is 27.

Assuming that there is only one blank between
the line number and the key word LET and only
one blank following that word, 27 print positions are needed to print the example statement.
The digit 3 is, therefore, printed in print
position 27.

The BASIC language assumes that there are five
zones on a sheet of output paper. These five
zones are divided this way:

    Zone 1,   print positions 1 - 15, inclusive
    Zone 2,   print positions 16 - 30, inclusive
    Zone 3,   print positions 31 - 45, inclusive
    Zone 4,   print positions 46 - 60, inclusive
    Zone 5,   print positions 61 - 72, inclusive

Study this next statement. What zone will the
value of R print in?

        1340   PRINT P, Q, R, S, T

179   All five zones

180   Zone 3

181   Zone 1

178

FRAME 178

You're close, but not quite right. Did you
observe that there is a blank ahead of and
following the word LET? The blanks must be
counted. When you count those blanks, the
digit "3" was found to be in print position
28.

Please go on to Frame 177.

FRAME 179

No, the value of R cannot print in all five zones. It may print in only one of them. Actually,

$$
\begin{aligned}
&P \text{ prints in Zone 1}\\
&Q \text{ prints in Zone 2}\\
&R \text{ prints in Zone 3}\\
&S \text{ prints in Zone 4}\\
&T \text{ prints in Zone 5}
\end{aligned}
$$

Please return to Frame 177 and make a better selection.

FRAME 180

Yes, the value of R prints in Zone 3.

The value of R will be left adjusted in
Zone 3. That is, the value last assigned
to R will be printed as far to the left as
possible in Zone 3. If R's value is -4.2,
for example, the minus sign will print at
print position 31. The remainder of the
number will print in print positions 32
through 34.

Suppose the value of R had been 4.2, what
print position would the 4 have printed in?
(You may have to use your intuition to answer this one correctly.)

182   31

183   32

184   It's really pretty random.   Anywhere
between 31 and 45.

FRAME 181

No, the value of P prints in Zone 1. We're
concerned with where the value of R prints.
If P prints in Zone 1, then Q prints in Zone
2, and R prints in Zone 3, etc.

Please return to Frame 177 and make a better
selection.

FRAME 182

No, the print position 31 will have something printed in it if the number being printed is negative. The number's minus sign will print there. If the number being printed is positive, print position 31 remains blank.

The correct response is that the "4" will appear in print position 32. Please proceed now to Frame 183.

FRAME 183

The digit prints in print position 32.

The system leaves print position 31 blank.
The rule is that when a value is negative, a
minus sign is placed in the left most print
position of a zone. If the value is positive,
a blank is left there. The number itself is
otherwise left adjusted.

Consider this next PRINT statement:

1745　PRINT G1, G5, G8

If G1's value is -29.6, the minus sign prints
in print position 1. If G5's value is 49.6,
the 4 prints in print position 17. If G8's
value is 764.23, what print position does the
7 print in?

185　23

186　31

187　32

FRAME 184

No, there's nothing random about the way this works. It works the same way every time. If a number to be printed is negative, a given print position (1, 16, 31, 46, 61) obtains a minus sign and the number itself follows. If the number is positive, those print positions are left blanks. The number follows.

Please go to Frame 183.

FRAME 185

No, you're not even close. The value of G8
must print in the third zone, print positions
31 through 45.

Please return to Frame 174 and proceed forward
again from that point.

FRAME 186

No, observe that 764.23 is a positive number.
It appears in Zone 3, print positions 31
through 45. Since print position 31 is re-
served for a negative number's minus sign,
the number we're discussing begins in print
position 32.

Please proceed now to Frame 187.

FRAME 187

The print position is 32.

If the value had been negative, the minus sign would have printed in print position 31.

If you write a PRINT statement in which semi-colons (;) are used between variable names rather than commas, the program will print requested values more tightly packed. Therefore, if your PRINT statement reads like this:

        1750   PRINT G1; G5; G8

The values last assigned to G1, G5, and G8 will be printed tightly packed on an output line. The system will automatically provide a blank between numbers.

Now study the next statement.

        1760   PRINT "TABLE OF COSTS"

Can you guess what the computer will do?

188   It will print the words TABLE OF COSTS beginning in print position 1.

189   It will print TABLE OF COSTS beginning in print position 13.

FRAME 188

The computer will print the words TABLE OF
COSTS beginning in print position 1. Any
literal messages that you want the computer
to print must be placed within quotation
marks. The quote marks will not be printed
when the statement is executed. Suppose you
want the computer to print END OF JOB beginning at print position 1. How would you
write the PRINT statement?

190   10 PRINT END OF JOB

191   10 PRINT "END OF JOB"

FRAME 189

No, the computer will print the words TABLE
OF COSTS beginning at print position 1. The
last letter S in COSTS will therefore print
at print position 14. There will be no quotes
in the printed message.

In the PRINT statement,

        1760   PRINT "TABLE OF COSTS"

the quotes surround the actual literal message
which is to be printed. The message printed
begins in print position 1 on the output paper
because there are no blanks shown between the
quotes and the letter T in table.

Please proceed now to Frame 188.

FRAME 190

No, the format of the PRINT statement must
be very closely followed. The statement
consists of a line number (10), the key
word (PRINT), and the message to be printed
which will appear between quotation marks.
To have the computer print END OF JOB, therefore, the correct PRINT statement has to be

        10   PRINT "END OF JOB"

When the computer executes this statement,
the message

            END OF JOB

begins at print position 1.

Please advance now to Frame 191.

FRAME 191

The statement would be written

      10   PRINT "END OF JOB"

The computer will begin the message in print position 1. If you want the message to begin in print position 2 you would write

      10   PRINT " END OF JOB"

Observe that there is a single blank inserted between the beginning quote marks and the letter E in END.

How many blanks would you place between the beginning quote marks and the letter E if you wanted the message to begin in print position 6?

192   6

193   5

FRAME 192

Your response is not correct. If you want
the letter E to print in print position 6,
there must be five blanks between the beginning quote marks and the letter E. The
message will then print according to this
table.

Character	Print Position
blank	1
blank	2
blank	3
blank	4
blank	5
E	6
N	7
D	8
etc.	etc.

Please proceed now to Frame 193.

FRAME 193

There would be five blanks ahead of the quote
marks. Each blank would occupy a print position
beginning with print position 1. The first
print position available for the letter E,
therefore, is print position 6.

In a print statement you may mix literal messages and the contents of variables. Example:

2005   PRINT "VALUE OF J ="; J

The computer will print VALUE OF J = beginning
in print position 1 of the output paper. Then
it will give the actual value last assigned to
J. Suppose the value of J is -32. In what
print position will the minus sign print?

194   14

195   1

196   31

FRAME 194

The minus sign will print in print position 14. The computer will print

        VALUE OF J = -32

The semicolon insures that the value of J will be printed tightly packed to the right of the message VALUE OF J =. However, the system does give one blank character automatically ahead of the numeric value. This fact explains the blank between the equal sign and the minus sign. Count the characters printed in the print positions beginning with print position 1. You'll see that the minus sign appears in print position 14.

Is this next BASIC statement valid? What would you guess?

    3080   PRINT "ALPHA =";A;" BETA =";B

197   Yes

198   No

FRAME 195

No, your answer is not at all correct. In print position 1 the letter V will print. You seem to have gotten off the track a bit.

Please return to Frame 183 and proceed from there.

FRAME 196

No, you seem to have mixed up the print
position of J's value with the second zone
of the output paper. If the semicolon in
the example had been a comma,

        2005   PRINT "VALUE OF J =",J

then the value of J will appear beginning in
print position 31, the beginning of the third
zone.

Please return to Frame 193 and see if you
can find a better selection.

FRAME 197

The answer is Yes.

The computer will print a line such as

    ALPHA =   8.945 BETA = -1.05

The exact values printed depend, of course,
upon what the actual values of A and B are.
The word ALPHA begins at print position 1.
There are two blanks following the first
equals sign, because A's value is positive.

In addition to the printing of literal messages and of values assigned to variables
you may ask the computer to print the result
of a calculation. Here is an example:

    8500   PRINT 77.4/2

What will the computer do?

199 It will print an error message.

200 It will print 38.7 beginning in print
     position 2.

FRAME 198

The statement may appear complex and possibly incorrect, but it is valid. The statement directs the computer to print the word ALPHA followed by the actual value assigned to A. Then the computer is directed to print the word BETA followed by the actual value assigned to B.

Observe that the statement directs a blank to be placed ahead of the letter B. The word BETA will thus be separated from A's actual value. Frame 197 shows what the printed line will look like. Please proceed to Frame 197.

FRAME 199

Sorry, your answer is not correct. The computer will first compute the result of 77.4
divided by 2, (38.7), then print that value
beginning at print position 2. The effect of
the statement is as if these two statements
had been written:

            8450   LET X = 77.4/2
            8500   PRINT X

The difference is that the statement

            8500   PRINT 77.4/2

computes and prints the answer, but it does
not save it for later use.

Please proceed to Frame 200.

FRAME 200

The computer will print 38.7 beginning in print position 2. The program computes 77.4/2, then prints the result. It prints the result in Zone 1. The expression you write may be as complicated as you wish. The expression may include parentheses. You may for example, enter this statement:

    1000   PRINT (A - B)/(C - D), P * 8/R,Q

(It is understood that values have been assigned to A, B, C, D, P, Q, and R earlier in the program). Observe that this statement causes three values to be printed. They are:

1. The result of calculation (A-B)/(C-D).

2. The result of calculation P*8/R.

3. The last value assigned to Q.

How many of the zones will receive a number?

201   8

202   3

203   1

FRAME 201

No, your response seems to be a poor guess.
You should review the fact that there are
five zones on output paper and that the PRINT
statement may place values in those zones.

Please return to Frame 177 and resume from
that point.

FRAME 202

Three zones will receive answers. The two calculated results go into Zones 1 and 2, respectively, and the value assigned to Q goes into the third zone.

When you ask the computer to make a calculation and print it, you may not also assign that value to a variable name. This next statement is wrong:

    1805   PRINT D = (4.6/A) -B

This statement attempts to be an assignment and a PRINT statement at the same time, which can't be done. How could you rewrite the statement?

204   1805 PRINT (4.6/A)-B

205   1805 LETPRINT (4.6/A)-B

FRAME 203

No, examine the statement and you will see
that it calls for three answers. The first
answer is given by (A - B)/(C - D), the
second by P*8/R, and the third by Q. The
PRINT statement gives these three terms separated by commas. The three values will require
three zones on the output paper.

Please proceed to Frame 202.

FRAME 204

Yes, your answer is correct:

1805   PRINT (4.6/A)-B

Of course the value 4.6/A-B has not been assigned to a variable name and therefore must be recomputed if the value is needed in a later portion of the program. Do not forget, though, that you can always <u>assign</u> in one statement and <u>print</u> in another. Example:

1804   LET D = (4.6/A)-B
1805   PRINT D

Employing a simple PRINT statement not followed by a literal value, a variable name or a calculation, causes a blank line to be printed. Example:

1806   PRINT

There is no response required for this frame. Please go on to Frame 206.

FRAME 205

No, your response is not very good. Your
basic understanding of assignment and PRINT
statements is weak. You should review the
material we have covered. We're sorry, but
you really ought to return to Frame 156 and
proceed from there. Please do so now.

FRAME 206

With only a knowledge of the LET, PRINT, and
END statements, you already know how to write
a wide variety of computer programs. Here is
an example of a program which is not as ele-
mentary as the ones we've discussed so far:

```
1000    LET D = SQR (7.4↑2 - 4*2.2*1.2)
1010    LET E = 2*2.2
1020    PRINT (-7.4+D)/E
1030    PRINT (-7.4-D)/E
1040    END
```

This program computes the roots of the quad-
ratic equation

$$R = \frac{-b \pm \sqrt{b^2 - 4ac}}{2a}$$

when a equals 2.2, b equals 7.4, and c equals
1.2. How many lines of output does this program print?

207   2

208   1

FRAME 207

The correct answer is 2.

The program prints two lines. There is one number per line printed in Zone 1. This program first computed $\sqrt{b^2 - 4ac}$ where a was 2.2 b was 7.4, and c was 1.2. The result of the calculation was assigned to D. Then 2a was computed. This result was assigned to E.

Finally, in order to compute and print two values of R, the program combined D and E with b according to the original equation. That is, R was computed twice. Once as

$$R = \frac{-b+D}{E}$$

and once as

$$R = \frac{-b - D}{E}$$

The program could have been written this way:

```
1000   PRINT (-7.4+SQR(7.4↑2-4*2.2*1.2))/(2*2.2)
1010   PRINT (-7.4-SQR(7.4↑2-4*2.2*1.2))/(2*2.2)
1021   END
```

209 A program should use as many statements as possible.

210 The second method is not as accurate as the first.

211 The second method is not as efficient as the first.

FRAME 208

No, the answer is not 1. There are two PRINT
statements in the program. The computer will
therefore print two lines of answers. The
value printed on the first line is the result
of

$$\frac{-7.4 + \sqrt{7.4^2 - 4 \times 2.2 \times 1.2}}{2 \times 2.2}$$

and on the second line,

$$\frac{-7.4 - \sqrt{7.4^2 - 4 \times 2.2 \times 1.2}}{2 \times 2.2}$$

Please proceed to Frame 207.

FRAME 209

No, the major concern should not be how many statements a program uses or how few. The major concern should be how efficient the program is. Since some of the same calculations were made twice, the program shown in Frame 207 is considered inefficient.

Please return to Frame 207 and make a better selection.

FRAME 210

No, the two programs are equally accurate.
Both programs make the same calculations.
The difference in the programs lies in the
fact that the second program repeats certain
calculations when it shouldn't have to.
The second program is therefore less efficient
than the first one.

Please return to Frame 207 and make a better
selection.

FRAME 211

The answer is the second method is not as efficient as the first.

The second version of the program makes several
calculations twice which is not necessary.
Despite the fact that the first program contains
more statements, it runs faster than the second
and therefore costs less.

In this example, the difference in cost between
the two programs is so small that you'd need a
microscope to see it. Nevertheless, one should
get into the habit of writing efficient programs.
Ultimately this habit will save the programmer
thousands of dollars over the length of his
career.

Now let's discuss the IF statement.

Here is an example:

        110   IF A = X THEN 500

What is the key word in this type of statement?

212   IF

213   THEN

FRAME 212

The key word is IF.

An IF statement enables a program to make a
test of a condition as it executes. Then,
the computer takes an action depending upon
the result of that test. Study this program:

```
35   LET N = 1
45   IF N > 3 THEN 85
55   PRINT "PLEASE CHECK STATUS"
65   LET N = N + 1
75   GO TO 45
85   PRINT "THANK YOU"
95   END
```

In this example N is a counter. N counts
the number of times that the computer has
printed PLEASE CHECK STATUS. See if you can
follow the program from start to finish.

How many times will the program cause that
message to be printed?

214   3

215   4

FRAME 213

No, if you recall from our discussion of the LET and PRINT statements, the key word of a statement is the first word. In an IF statement, therefore, you would expect the key word to be IF.

Please proceed to Frame 212.

FRAME 214

The message is printed three times.

The program establishes a counter. The name of the counter may be any legal name the programmer selects. In this example, the name of the counter is N.

N is initially set to 1. Then it is checked to determine whether it is greater than (>) 3. If yes, the program jumps to the statement at line 85. If not, the program goes on to the next statement in sequence and, in this example, prints PLEASE CHECK STATUS.

What is the value of the counter N, when the message is printed for the first time?

216   1

217   2

FRAME 215

No, your answer is incorrect.

In order to understand this program you need
to know that the symbol > means "greater than."
So long as N is not greater than 3, the computer will print PLEASE CHECK STATUS.

An IF statement always tests a condition.
(In this case, N > 3). If the condition is
true, the program takes the indicated jump
(in this case to line 85). When the condition
is false, the program goes to the next statement in sequence (in this case to line 55).

Follow the program step by step and you will
see that the message is printed 3 times.
Please go to Frame 214 for an additional explanation.

FRAME 216

N's value is 1.

The first value of the counter (N) is 1.
Then the program increases N by 1. This
is done at line 65. The statement

$$65 \quad \text{LET } N = N + 1$$

means add 1 to N. (The old value of N plus
1 replaces the old value and becomes the new
value of N.)

The GO TO statement at line 75 tells the program to return unconditionally to line 45.
There, N is checked again to determine whether
it is greater than 3. It isn't. N's value
is 2 so the message PLEASE CHECK STATUS is
printed again.

What is the value of N when the message is
printed for the second time?

218   2

219   3

FRAME 217

No, your answer is incorrect. Examine the
program and you will see that the counter's
value (N) is initially set to 1. Then, since
N is not greater than 3, the computer prints
PLEASE CHECK STATUS for the first time.

When the message is printed for the first time,
therefore, N's value is not 2. It actually is
1.

Please proceed now to Frame 216.

FRAME 218

The correct answer is 2.

You can see that the value of the counter keeps in step with the number of times the message has been printed. When N is 3, the message prints for the third time. When N is 4, the program does not print the message for the fourth time. When N is 4, the IF statement finds that N's value is greater than 3. Therefore the GO TO 85 option in the IF statement is taken. The program jumps to line 85 which causes the program to print THANK YOU, then end.

How would you change line 45 if you want the computer to print the CHECK STATUS message 100 times?

220   IF N > 99 THEN 85

221   IF N > 100 THEN 85

FRAME 219

No, read Frame 212 again. N's value is in-
creased to 2. Then the value is checked to
determine whether that value is greater than
3. Since it isn't,the message is printed.
The message is printed at once before N has
a chance to change. Therefore, when N's value
is 2, the computer prints PLEASE CHECK STATUS
for the second time.

Please advance now to Frame 218.

FRAME 220

No, you will be one off. Study the program
in Frame 212 again. The IF statement is
written so that it tests N to see if it is
greater than 3. When N is greater than 3,
the computer has printed the CHECK STATUS
message thru logic. Logic tells you that
when N is greater than 100, the computer
has printed the message 100 times.

The correct answer to the problem is, therefore,

IF N > 100 THEN 85

Please go now to Frame 221.

FRAME 221

The statement to use is

       IF N > 100 THEN 85

The IF statement offers a number of different
ways that it may be written. Here are some:

       400   IF B = F   THEN 700
       410   IF C > L   THEN 800
       420   IF 6 < D   THEN 900
       430   IF M > =   P * R THEN 1000
       440   IF (N-P)/T = U + V THEN 1100
       450   IF V < = 17 THEN 1200
       460   IF W < > THEN 1300

The symbol = means equals; the symbol > means
greater than; the symbol < means less than.
Can you determine what the symbols > = mean?

222   Greater than.

223   Greater than or equals.

224   Less than or equals.

FRAME 222

No, > = does not mean greater than. You over-
looked the equals (=) sign. Please return to
Frame 221 and make a better selection.

FRAME 223

The answer is greater than or equal.

The two symbols typed one after the other means greater than or equal.

Similarly,<= means less than or equal and <> means not equal.

In all IF statements a condition is tested to determine what the relationship is between one value and another. When the condition tested is found to be true, the program makes the indicated jump.

Example:

        15   IF P > 17.4   THEN 300

If P is greater than 17.4 the program jumps to line 300. Where does the program go if P is not greater than 17.4?

225   To the beginning of the program.

226   To the next line of the program.

FRAME 224

You're almost right. The symbol > does not
mean less than; it means greater than.

Now, if the IF statement shows a greater
than symbol <u>and</u> an equals symbol, the IF
statement must be checking whether one value
is greater than or equal to the other.

Example:

        40   IF (X > = Y) THEN 2000

The computer will jump to line 200 if X's
value is actually greater than or equal to
Y's value. If X's value is less than Y's
value, the computer will go to the next
statement of the program.

Please return to Frame 221 and make a better
selection.

FRAME 225

Your reply is not correct. The computer always
checks to see if a condition being tested is
true. If it is, the computer jumps to the
line number given after the word THEN. If
the condition is not true, the program goes
to the next statement in sequence.

Please return now to Frame 223 and make another selection.

FRAME 226

Correct, the program goes to the next line of the program. The symbols =, > , < , > =, < = and <> are called relational symbols. You may place an actual number, a BASIC variable name, or expression on either side of the relational symbols. The resulting condition is tested to determine whether it is true or false. The word THEN immediately precedes the line number which tells the program where to go if the condition being tested is true.

What is wrong with this IF statement?

$$60 \quad IF \ G < H \ LINE \ 300$$

227 The word LINE must be THEN.

228 G can never be less than H.

229 An actual number must be shown at the left of the less than symbol.

FRAME 227

Yes, the word LINE must be THEN.

Study this additional example program.

```
100   LET P = 1000
110   LET Y = 1
120   IF Y > 10 THEN 180
130   LET I = .075 * P
140   PRINT Y, P, I
150   LET P = P + I
160   LET Y = Y + 1
170   GO TO 120
180   END
```

The program establishes a principle amount of $1000 to be invested at 7 1/2%. The interest is computed once a year for 10 years. Each year the computed interest is added to the old principle, thus creating a new principle.

The program prints 10 lines. On each line the year, principle and interest earned is printed.

There is no response required for this frame. Please proceed to Frame 230.

FRAME 228

No, you're not correct. G's value can
certainly be less than the value of H. If
G <u>is</u> less than H, the program will jump to
line 300; otherwise the computer will go to
the next statement in sequence.

Please return to Frame 226 and make a better
selection.

FRAME 229

No, Frame 226 clearly tells that actual
numbers, variable names, or expressions may
be shown on either side of relational symbols.
Therefore, G may appear on the left of the
less than symbol.

Please return to Frame 226 and make a better
selection.

FRAME 230

The IF statement is called a "conditional
jump" statement, because the flow of the
program execution is altered conditionally
when an IF statement is encountered.

For instance, in

1950 IF X<= R THEN 285

The program jumps to line 285 only if the
current value of X is less than or equal to
the current value of R. If the condition
being tested is not true; that is, if X is
larger than R, the program goes to the next
statement in sequence.

If an IF statement is an example of a conditional jump, what is an example of an unconditional jump to line 95?

231 600 IF 6 < 7 THEN 95.

232 GO TO 95.

FRAME 231

No, an unconditional jump is not an IF statement, because an IF statement is always a
conditional jump. It's true that the IF
statement given will cause the computer to
jump to line number 95, but the use of IF
statements is going at it the hard way.

Please return to Frame 230 to see if you can
find an easy way to accomplish the required
jump.

FRAME 232

Yes, your answer, GO TO 95, is correct.

It's true that the IF statement offered will cause an eventual jump to line 95, but an IF statement is definitely conditional. The program does check 6 to determine whether it is less than 7. (Of course it is.) But a programmer should never write a conditional statement if he knows ahead of time how the computer will always respond to it. A simple GO statement is the correct statement to use. A GO TO is an unconditional jump.

No response required to this frame. Congratulations for having successfully completed Section IV.

SECTION V

LOOPS

FRAME 233

The ability to use conditional and unconditional statements permits you to instruct the computer to perform "loops." A loop is a series of statements executed more than once. For instance, we may have a program like this:

```
100    LET Q = 1
110    IF Q > 100 THEN 150
120    PRINT Q, LOG(Q)
130    LET Q = Q + 1
140    GO TO 110
150    END
```

This program is very similar to one we showed in the last section. It prints 100 lines. Each line contains a value of Q and Q's natural log.

Would you say that this program incorporates a loop?

234 Yes

235 No

236 Depends upon how soon Q becomes greater than 100.

FRAME 234

Yes, the program does incorporate a loop.

You can see that when Q, a counter, equals 1, the statements at lines 110, 120, 130, and 140 will be executed for the first time. When Q equals 2, those statements will be executed for a second time, etc. When Q equals 100, the statements will be executed for the 100th and last time. Observe that Q, the counter, is used as an actual value at line 120 where its log is computed. In a loop, a counter is initialized only once.

A loop consists of four parts:

1. Initialization of counter.
2. Test of counter.
3. Body of loop.
4. Increment or decrement of counter and transfer back to test of counter.

In a loop, how many times is the counter initialized?

237   Once for each time the body is executed.

238   Only once.

FRAME 235

No, your answer is incorrect.

The program does include a loop. A loop is a series of statements executed more than once. In the program the statements at lines 110, 120, 130, and 140 are executed several times. The statements taken as a group form a loop.

Please proceed to Frame 234.

FRAME 236

No, your answer is incorrect. Whether or
not there is a loop in the program does not
depend upon how soon Q exceeds 100.

There definitely is a loop in the program.
The statements at lines 110, 120, 130, and
140 constitute a loop. The value of Q
changes gradually, a unit at a time. Therefore to predict when Q will be greater than
100 is easy.

Frame 234 gives additional information concerning the loop in this program. Please
go there now and study it carefully.

FRAME 237

No, please reread Frame 234, which clearly
says that the counter in a loop is executed
only once. In the example program, Q is the
counter with an initial value of 1. That
value is given to the counter only once.

Please proceed to Frame 238.

FRAME 238

The counter Q is initialized only once.

Study this program skeleton.

```
100   LET D = 1
110   IF D > 2000 THEN 190
120 -
130 -
140 -
150 -
160 -
170   LET D = D + 1
180   GO TO 110
190   END
```

What is the name of the counter?

239 D

240 We cannot tell, because it is shown
     somewhere between lines 120 and 160
     inclusive.

FRAME 239

Yes, the name of the counter is D. It is initialized at line 100 with the value 1. The
statement at line 100, therefore, contains
the initialization part of the loop.

At what line is the counter tested for the
maximum time the loop is to be executed?

241   170

242   110

FRAME 240

No, your answer indicates you have a very
poor understanding of what we have said so
far in this section. The name of the counter
in the program is D. It is a variable name
which counts from 1 on up in steps of 1.

Frame 233 gives a program with a counter
named Q. Please return to that frame and
resume from that point.

FRAME 241

No, your response is quite incorrect. In
order to test a counter, an IF statement must
be used. In Frame 238 the IF statement which
checks counter D is located at line 110.
There the program tests D to determine whether
its value is greater than 2000.

You should make a fresh start in this section.
Please return to Frame 233 and note the IF
statement at line 110. The value of the
counter Q is tested there. Resume studying
from that frame.

FRAME 242

You're correct. The counter is tested at line 110.

The IF statement at line 110 checks to determine whether the value of D exceeds 2000. If it does, the program has executed the body of the loop 2000 times and should be terminated. Therefore, the program jumps to the END statement at line 190 only when the program has executed the required loop the desired number of times.

In this example, what statement or statements constitute the body of the loop?

243   The statement at line 100.

244   The statements between lines 120 and 160 inclusive.

FRAME 243

No, the body of a loop is not the statement
where a counter is initialized. You have
missed the fact that the body of the loop
must be the statements at lines 120 through
160.

Keep in mind that there are four parts to a
loop: Initialization; Body; Augment; and
Test. Often by a process of elimination
you can determine which part is being discussed.

Please return to Frame 233 and proceed from
there.

FRAME 244

Correct! The body of the loop is formed by
the statements between lines 120 and 160 inclusive.

There can be as many statements as you require
in the body of a loop. Those statements may
include assignment (LET) statements, PRINT
statements, IF statements, and others.
Later in this section we'll give an example
of how IF statements may be used in the body
of a loop.

At line 170 of the example is shown the part
of a loop which changes the counter. The
value 1 is being added to the counter. At
line 180 an unconditional jump directs the
program to go back to the part of a loop
which tests the counter.

There is no response required for this frame.

Please proceed now with Frame 245.

FRAME 245

Two special BASIC statements are provided to help you write loops. Study these side-by-side examples:

```
100   LET V = 1              100   FOR V = 1 TO 250
110   IF V > 250 THEN 170
120 -                        120 -
130 -                        130 -
140 -                        140 -
150   LET V = V + 1          150   NEXT V
160   GO TO 110
170   END                    170   END
```

The program on the left requires more statements to set up than the one on the right, but both programs accomplish exactly the same task.

How many statements are there in the body of both loops?

246   3

247   8

248   5

FRAME 246

The body of both loops consists of three statements. This number is a constant for both programs.

In the right hand program the FOR statement assigns an initial value to the named counter (V) and determines whether V exceeds the maximum value that the counter may have. The FOR statement shows that the maximum value that the counter may have is 250.

The FOR statement, therefore, initializes a counter and checks it for a maximum value. What statement adds 1 to the counter?

249 The NEXT statement.

250 A statement in the body of the loop.

251 None. The counter's value remains constant at 1.

FRAME 247

No, eight is not correct. You apparently
have counted the statements in the entire
program. There are eight statements, but not
all of them constitute the body of the loop.
At line 100 for example, the counter is initialized. At various other lines, the counter
is augmented and tested. These actions happen outside the loop.

Please return to Frame 245 and make a better
selection.

FRAME 248

No, 5 is not correct. To determine which
statements constitute the body of a loop,
study the given program to determine which
statements are being executed over and over.
In the example, the statements being executed
250 times are those between lines 120 and 140
inclusive.

Please return to Frame 245 and make a better
selection.

FRAME 249

The NEXT statement adds 1 to the counter,
then returns to the FOR statement - that portion
of the statement where the counter's value
is compared with the maximum value that the
counter may have.

FOR and NEXT statements work as a team. For
every FOR statement, you will find an associated NEXT statement and vice versa.

You can see that the use of FOR/NEXT statements enables you to write loops more easily.
Do FOR and NEXT loops employ the four parts
of loops listed earlier?

252   No, because the loops are simplified.

253   Yes.

FRAME 250

No, a statement in the body of the loop
does not add one to the counter. Look at
the program. You can see that the name of
the counter is V, which obtains an initial
value at line 100 of both programs. In the
left program the statement at line 150

150   LET V = V + 1

causes 1 to be added to V. What statement
in the right program accomplishes the same
task. Please return to Frame 246 and make
a better selection.

FRAME 251

No, a counter's value cannot remain constant.
You have apparently missed the importance of
counters in the two programs in Frames 233
and 238. Please return to Frame 233 and begin this section all over again.

252

FRAME 252

Sorry, the answer is Yes. Despite the fact
that FOR/NEXT loops look simpler than loops
which explicitly show all four parts, FOR/
NEXT loops do employ the four parts of loops:
Initialization; Body; Augment; and Test.
Some of the parts are hidden. For example,
in

        100   FOR D = 1 to 200

                  .
                  .
                  .

        175   NEXT D

the initialization and testing of the counter
are given where the FOR statement is located.
The augmenting is done at the point where the
NEXT statement is located and the body of the
loop is between the FOR and NEXT statements.

Please proceed now to Frame 253.

FRAME 253

The answer to the question is Yes, the four
parts are present.

Regardless of whether a programmer writes a
loop using explicit parts of loops or whether
he writes a loop using FOR and NEXT statements, the four parts of a loop are always
present. The FOR statement takes care of two
parts: the initialization and the test of
the counter. The NEXT statement takes care
of the augmenting the counter. The body of
the loop, of course, lies between the FOR
and NEXT statements.

When you write a FOR statement, you have a
great deal of freedom in how you may write
it. Here's an example:

        300 FOR H = 3 TO 214 STEP 10

What is the name of the counter?

254 FOR

255 H

FRAME 254

No, your answer is incorrect. FOR is a word
which precedes the name of the counter.
From our discussion of FOR/NEXT loops, it
should be clear that the name of the counter
is H.

You need a new start in understanding how
FOR/NEXT loops are formed. To do this,
please return to Frame 245 and proceed.

FRAME 255

Yes, the name of the counter is H. The variable H begins with a count of 3 and advances
toward 214. In advancing toward 214, the
value of the counter jumps in steps of 10.
This means that the counter's value is first
3, then 13, then 23, etc.

In this example, what is the initial value
assigned to the counter?

256   3

257   214

FRAME 256

The initial value assigned to the counter is 3. That initial value can be any value you select - either whole number or mixed, either positive or negative.

In this example, what is the value the counter advances toward?

258 214

259 10

260 -214

FRAME 257

No, you didn't read Frame 255 carefully. The
initial value assigned to the counter is 3,
not 214. The counter advances toward the
value 214. The value 10 represents what is
added to the counter each time it changes.

The counter's initial value is 3. As the
loop is executed, subsequent values become
13, 23, 33, 43, etc.

Please proceed now to Frame 256.

FRAME 258

The counter moves toward the value 214.
Actually the counter never gets there,
because of the step size given.

The FOR statement shows STEP 10. This
means that the counter's value increases in
steps of 10. In the example the final value
attained by the counter is 213.

What does STEP 10 mean?

261   Every time the counter is changed,
      it increases by 10.

262   The program must slow down so that
      each step may be studied.

FRAME 259

No, the value 10 is the step size. Whenever
the counter's value increases, it does so by
the value given as the step size.

The counter advances toward the value 214.

Please proceed to Frame 258.

FRAME 260

No, not at all! Where did you get -214?
Look at the FOR statement in Frame 253.
This frame clearly shows that the FOR state-
ment is:

        300   FOR H = 3 TO 214 STEP 10

The counter advances in steps of 10 toward
the value 214. Every time the body of the
loop is executed, H changes. The values H
attains are: 3, 13, 23, 33, 43, etc. all
the way up to and including 213.

Please proceed now to Frame 258.

FRAME 261

Correct! Every time the counter is changed,
it increases by 10.

If no step size is shown in a FOR statement,
the assumed value of the step size is 1.
In the example, the value of the counter increases by 10 every time it changes. This
means that as the program executes, the value
of the counter will be

3, 13, 23, 33, 43, 53, 63, 73, 83, 93, 103,
113, 123, 133, 143, 153, 163, 173, 183, 193,
203, and 213.

Observe that the program does not use 223 in
the body of the loop since 223 is larger than
214. (214 is the maximum value for H shown
in the FOR statement.)

How many times will the body of the loop be
executed?

263   213 or 214

264   22

FRAME 262

No, your answer is pure guesswork. And it's wrong. Somewhere along the line you became confused. Back up a bit and return to Frame 233. Resume from that point.

FRAME 263

No, 213 and 214 are too large. If the step
size was 1, then the body of the loop would
be executed 214 times, because the counter's
value would range from 1 to 214 in steps of
1. But the step size is not 1; it is 10.
To determine how many times the body of the
loop will be executed, you can simply count
the number of different values H will attain.
These values are given in Frame 261.

Please return to Frame 261 and make a better
selection.

FRAME 264

Yes, the loop will be executed 22 times.

The counter H will take on 22 values, which begin at 3 and go up in steps of 10 through 213.

Now consider this problem. Suppose you need to obtain the square root of all values from 21 through 120 in steps of 11. The program you would write is this:

```
100    FOR W = 21 TO 120 STEP 11
200    PRINT W, SQR(W)
300    NEXT W
400    END
```

This program prints several lines of answers. Each line gives the value of W and the square root of W. How many lines of output will the program give?

265   10

266   12

FRAME 265

The program will print 10 lines. The counter
W will have an initial value of 21 and will
then increase by 11 every time the body of
the loop is executed. The actual values
which the counter attains and uses in the
body of the loop are: 21, 32, 43, 54, 65,
76, 87, 98, 109, and 120. Would the program
have worked exactly the same way if the FOR
statement had read:

       100   FOR W = 21 TO 121 STEP 11

or

       100   FOR W = 21 TO 130 STEP 11

267   Yes.

268   No.

269   The chances are against it.

FRAME 266

No, you're just a bit off. The body of the loop will be executed 10 times. The value of the counter during those executions will be: 21, 32, 43, 54, 65, 76, 87, 98, 109, and 120.

Please proceed to Frame 265.

FRAME 267

The answer is Yes. The last value actually
used when assigned to W is 120.

The next value that the counter could possibly
attain is 131. Since the last value which
the counter has been permitted to attain is
120 (which is less than 131), the program will
not execute the body of the loop for an 11th
time. It will execute the body of the loop
for the last time when W is 120.

FOR statements may also be written this way:

```
1000    FOR A = 1.6 TO 9.4 STEP .8
1010    FOR B = C TO 8.9 STEP .4
1020    FOR C = D TO E STEP 5
1030    FOR D = E TO F STEP G
```

The examples show that beginning and ending
values for the counter may be actual numbers
or BASIC names.

How many times will the loop, controlled by
the FOR statement at line 1030, be executed?

270   10 times.

271   This can't be determined, since we
      haven't been told what values were
      last assigned to E, F, and G.

FRAME 268

Your answer is not correct. If the FOR
statement is:

        100   FOR W = 21 TO 121 STEP 11

the actual values which W attains are: 21,
32, 43, 54, 65, 76, 87, 98, 109, and 120.

And if the FOR statement is

        100   FOR W = 21 TO 130 STEP 11

the actual values which W attains are: 21,
32, 43, 54, 65, 76, 87, 98, 109, and 120.

The body of the loop executes 10 times, the
same as when the FOR statement is

        100   FOR W = 21 TO 120 STEP 11

Please proceed now to Frame 267.

FRAME 269

Your answer is incorrect and indicates that
a review is in order. Please return to Frame
233 and proceed from there.

FRAME 270

No, there is no basis at all for the answer
you have selected. Possibly you felt that
the answer given as the second choice in
Frame 267 couldn't be right. It is right,
though. It is not possible to determine
how many times the loop will be executed,
because there is no hint as to the values
actually held by E, F, and G.

In order to answer the question correctly,
you must have the information. Please go to
Frame 271.

FRAME 271

The answer to this question can't be determined since we haven't been told what values were last assigned to E, F, and G.

The three values given in a FOR statement may be whole numbers or mixed numbers. They may be actual numbers, names, or even expressions. Here's an example using expressions for all three values:

    800 FOR I = A * B TO C / D STEP E + F

Values, of course, must have been assigned earlier to A, B, C, D, E, and F.

Would you say that some of those three values may be negative?

272 Yes.

273 No.

274 This feature is not yet available, but will be included in a year.

FRAME 272

Yes, one or more of the three values shown
in a FOR statement may be negative.

Study these examples:

```
1200   FOR J = -10 TO 20 STEP 2
1300   FOR K = -20 TO -80 STEP -5
1400   FOR L = 90 TO 10 STEP -10
```

Care should be taken to insure that the program will eventually leave the loop. In the
statement at line 1300, for example, the
program can vary from -20 to -80 in steps of
5 units if the step size is -5. If the step
size is 5, the program will add to -20 rather
than subtract from it. The loop will never
terminate.

Is the next FOR statement valid? What would
you guess?

```
8000   FOR M = 14 TO 14
```

275   Yes.

276   Only if the NEXT statement follows
      immediately.

FRAME 273

Your answer is incorrect. Some of the values in a FOR statement may be negative. This next FOR statement is OK as an example:

700   FOR K = -40 TO -30 STEP .5

The program assigns the values: -40, -39.5, -39, etc. to K. In all there are 21 values assigned to K. The last one being -30.

Please go on to Frame 272.

FRAME 274

No, your answer indicates that you are
either kidding or have not read the text
carefully. If you're only joking, please
return to Frame 271 and make another selection. If you're serious, you need a thorough
review of FOR and NEXT loops. Please return
to Frame 245 and resume from that point.

FRAME 275

Yes, the statement is valid.

When the FOR statement sets a counter to some value, it is immediately checked to determine if it exceeds the maximum value indicated. If not, the program executes the required loop. Therefore, in

8000   FOR M = 14 to 14

the program will assign 14 to M, then the program will execute the loop once. Having done so, the program will add 1 to M making it 15. Since 15 is larger than 14, the program will stop executing the loop. The program will then jump to the statement following the next M statement.

Do you remember what was said about the body of a loop? Can you have an IF statement in the body of a loop?

277   Yes, but the IF will act like GO TO.

278   Yes, any BASIC statement except END may be used in the body of a loop.

FRAME 276

No, your answer is incorrect. It's true
that we're asking you to guess what the
answer is, but you should be able to choose
the correct answer through a process of elimination.

What good would it do, for instance, if a
NEXT statement immediately followed the FOR
statement? There would be no loop. The
most reasonable guess is that the FOR statement is all right and that the body of the
loop would be executed once or twice. Actually, once is correct.

Please go to Frame 275 for an additional
explanation of why the statement is valid.

FRAME 277

You're partly right. The computer will indeed accept an IF statement in the body of a
loop. But the second part of your answer is
not right. In a loop, an IF statement works
in the usual way. A condition is tested and
the program either makes a jump or proceeds
to the next statement in sequence.

In Frame 278 an example is given showing how
an IF statement may be effectively used in
the body of a loop. Please go there now.

FRAME 278

An IF statement may be used in the body of
a loop. In fact, any BASIC statement except
END may be used in the body.

As an example of how an IF statement may be
used in the body of a loop, let's consider
an investing problem. Suppose a person
wants to find out how many years it will
take to double an investment at an interest
rate of 6% per year compounded once a year.

The programmer could write the program this
way:

```
1000   LET P = 1
1100   FOR K = 1 TO 100
1200   LET P = P + .06 * P
1300   IF P>=2 THEN 1700
1400   NEXT K
1500   PRINT "INVESTMENT DID NOT DOUBLE"
1600   GO TO 1800
1700   PRINT "INVESTMENT DOUBLED",K
1800   END
```

How much money is this individual investing?

279   $100

280   $1

FRAME 279

No, the actual value being invested is $1.
At line 1000, the value 1 is assigned to P.
The problem is to determine how long it will
take an investment to double. The answer will
be the same regardless of whether 1 is assigned
to P or 1,000,000.

Please proceed to Frame 280.

FRAME 280

The investment is $1.

In the program P means principle. In order
to find the answer, the value of P does not
matter. The answer will be the same whether
P is 1 or 1,000,000.

The FOR statement has been set up to cycle
through 100 years of investing. Everyday
experience tells us that the money will
double long before the 100 years are up.
That's where the IF statement comes in. As
soon as P is greater than 2, the principle
has more than doubled and the value of K
tells how many years are required.

What does line 1200 in the program accomplish?

281　It computes the interest at 6% for one
　　　year.

282　It computes the interest at 6% for one
　　　year and adds it to whatever value P
　　　currently has.

283　It computes the interest at 6% and checks
　　　it to determine whether it appears legal.

FRAME 281

This is only part of the answer. The program does more than just compute the interest. Study the line 1200 again and see if you can make a better response.

Please return to Frame 280.

FRAME 282

Correct. The program computes the interest at 6% for one year and adds it to whatever value P currently has.

Each year the value of P is compounded by adding the interest earned in the last year. In the program what would happen if the GO TO statement at line 1600 were not there and the program somehow jumped to line 1500?

284 The program would print INVESTMENT DID NOT DOUBLE, then it would immediately print INVESTMENT DOUBLED. The two lines would be contradictory.

285 The program would print INVESTMENT DID NOT DOUBLE, then it would continue the program until the investment doubled.

FRAME 283

The program does indeed compute interest at
6%, but it does nothing to check the result to
see if it is legal. Please study line 1200
again. Then make a better selection.

Please return to Frame 280.

FRAME 284

Correct!
The program would print INVESTMENT DID NOT
DOUBLE, then it would immediately print
INVESTMENT DOUBLED. The two lines would be
contradictory.

Of course when the interest rate is 6%, the
program should never get to line 1500. It
will eventually jump to line 1700. But suppose you change the rate of interest to 1/4 of
1% compounded annually. Would the $1 invest-
ment double within 100 years? It wouldn't,
and the program would cycle through 100 years
of compounding, eventually reaching line 1500
of the program. The program would print the
two messages mentioned above. The GO TO at
line 1600 is definitely needed.

No response required for this frame. Congratulations upon having completed Section V.

FRAME 285

No, you didn't follow the program carefully.
Please go back to the program shown in Frame
278. Assume the program was unable to double
P in 100 years (because of a very low interest
rate), the program would print the message
shown at line 1500. Then what would it do?

Please return to Frame 282 and make another
selection.

SECTION VI

INPUT DATA

FRAME 286

In this section we will discuss three types
of statements which permit even greater flex-
ibility when writing BASIC programs. They
are INPUT, READ, and DATA. The INPUT statement enables you to converse directly with
your program instead of only with the time
sharing system. Here's an example:

```
100    PRINT "HOW MUCH IS 6 * 8?"
110    INPUT A
120    IF A = 48 THEN 150
130    PRINT "NO, THAT'S WRONG.  TRY AGAIN."
140    GO TO 100
150    PRINT "CORRECT!"
160    END
```

How long will this program run?

287   It depends upon how soon the user
      gives the correct answer.

288   It will run all day, because there's
      an endless loop in the program.

289   Not long. The user gets only one
      chance to give a correct answer.

FRAME 287

Your answer is correct.

How long the program will run depends upon
how soon the user gives the correct answer.

When the program is executed, the system types
a question mark (?) on the output paper. The
user must then type a number. This number
will be accepted as the answer to the question:
HOW MUCH IS 6 * 8? That answer is assigned
to variable A. Then A is checked to determine
whether or not it equals 48. If so, the program types CORRECT!

What happens if the input answer is not 48?

290   The program types NO, THAT'S WRONG,
      then the program stops.

291   The program types NO, THAT'S WRONG,
      then the program gives the user a
      chance to try again.

FRAME 288

No, your answer is not correct. The program
will not run all day, though it could. Observe that if the user types a correct answer, the program will print CORRECT! and
then stop.

Please return to Frame 286 and make another
selection.

FRAME 289

Sorry, your answer is not right. The program could run for a long long time. Observe that if the user types in a wrong answer, the program will give the user another chance. There is no limit to the number of chances the user may get. The program could run all day.

Please return to Frame 286 and make another selection.

FRAME 290

No, if you'll examine the program carefully
you'll see that the program does not do what
you have suggested.

Please study the program again and give a
better answer to the question in Frame 287.

FRAME 291

Correct!

The program types NO, THAT'S WRONG, then gives the user a chance to try again.

This program does indeed have an endless loop. The user could keep the program going all day provided he keeps giving wrong answers. If he gives the correct answer at once, though, the program types CORRECT, then stops.

When the program runs, the user would see this output:

```
HOW MUCH IS 6 * 8?
49
NO THAT'S WRONG.  TRY AGAIN.
HOW MUCH IS 6 * 8?
42
NO THAT'S WRONG.  TRY AGAIN.
HOW MUCH IS 6 * 8?
48
CORRECT!
```

Which line would you change if you did not want the program to keep repeating the question HOW MUCH IS 6 * 8?

292   140

293   110

FRAME 292

Line 140 would be the one to change.

If line 140 is changed to read

         140   GO TO 110

the program will only type the question once.
From that point on the program will jump
directly to the INPUT statement. Line 100
will thus be bypassed and the question in
that statement will not be repeated.

If a program is in an endless loop, you may
stop the execution of the program by depressing the key labeled BREAK. Be careful,
though. You cannot cause a program to resume from the point it stopped. If you type
RUN again, the program will begin the program from the beginning.

Do you think this next INPUT statement is
valid?

         200   INPUT J, K, L

294 Yes. The computer expects you to type
    in 3 numbers.

295 No, there's never any need to input
    more than one number at a time.

296 Yes, but it would be better to type
    three INPUT statements in a row.

FRAME 293

No, you've given the wrong line number. The
correct line number is 140. At that point
there is a statement reading

     140   GO TO 100

If you were to change that statement to

     140   GO TO 110

the program would bypass the question and
immediately type a question mark.

Please proceed now to Frame 292.

FRAME 294

Correct!

The answer is Yes. You may type a statement
which expects you to type in 3 numbers.

When the computer executes the INPUT statement, it types a question mark on the paper.
You must then type three numbers separated
by commas. Like this:

>   ?   15, 46, 8

The three values are assigned to J, K and L
and the program continues. If the numbers
you type don't agree with the INPUT statement, the computer automatically asks you to
repeat the input.

An input statement may require as many values
to be typed as required by the program. For
example:

>   850   INPUT P, Q, R, S, T

requires the typing in of 5 values separated
by commas.

No response is required for this frame.

Please proceed to Frame 297.

FRAME 295

Your answer is not correct. An INPUT statement may ask for more than one value. If you
enter

        200   INPUT J,K,L

the program expects three values to be typed.
If you enter

        200   INPUT J,K,L,M

the program expects four values to be typed,
etc.

There is therefore often a need to enter more
than one value through the use of an INPUT
statement.

Please return now to Frame 292 and make a
better selection.

FRAME 296

No, typing three input statements would not be better, because this is awkward and time consuming. You can do this:

```
200    INPUT J
201    INPUT K
202    INPUT L
```

This will cause three interruptions of the program where values are requested. If you type:

```
200    INPUT J,K,L
```

the computer will make only one interruption and will expect you to type in three values.

Please return to Frame 292 and make a better selection.

FRAME 297

Here is another program that shows how the INPUT statement may be used as a teaching tool.

```
1000   PRINT "THIS PROGRAM MULTIPLIES"
1010   PRINT "PLEASE TYPE IN 2 NUMBERS"
1020   INPUT P,R
1030   IF P = 0 THEN 1060
1040   PRINT P, R, P * R
1050   GO TO 1010
1060   END
```

How may a user stop this program when he has finished?

298   Hang up the phone.

299   After the computer types a question mark, type in two zeroes separated by commas.

FRAME 298

True, your action will stop the program,
but is a crude way of doing so. Instead
type in a value which the program will
check for. Observe that the program will
stop when the value zero is entered for P.

When the computer types a question mark,
you should therefore type two zeroes, one
for P and one for R. The program will sub-
sequently discover that P's value is zero
and the program will stop. (You must type
two zeroes since the INPUT statement expects
two zeroes.)

Please proceed now to Frame 299.

FRAME 299

The user may stop the program by typing in
two zeroes separated by commas. This is done
after the computer types a question mark.

To review, the program requests the user to
type in two numbers, multiplies them, and
then prints out a line of answers. Then the
program repeats the cycle. The cycle continues until the user types zero for P. There
is no endless loop in this program - it stops
when the key value, zero, is typed for P.

If the user wishes to give the program all the
numbers that it will require as the program
executes, he may employ the DATA statement.
Here is an example of such a statement:

10000   DATA 5, 9, 17, 8, 2, 16, 7, 13, 1, 0, 0

No response is required for this frame.

Please proceed to Frame 300.

FRAME 300

Values may be obtained from the DATA statement by means of the READ statement. Study
this example:

```
10000    DATA 5,9,17,8,2,16,7,13,1,44,6,7,0,0
10100    READ P, R
10200    IF P = 0 THEN 10500
10300    PRINT P, R, P * R
10400    GO TO 10100
10500    END
```

This program uses the READ statement rather
than the INPUT statement to obtain values to
work with.

How many lines of answers will this program
give?

301   None since the INPUT statement is
      missing.

302   6

303   7

FRAME 301

No, you missed the point. DATA and READ
statements may be used to <u>replace</u> INPUT statements. The program obtains 7 sets of values
from the DATA statement. Six of those sets
are actually procesed - the 7th set is used
to provide a sentinel value for P.

Please return to Frame 300 and make another
selection.

FRAME 302

The program prints 6 lines of answers since
there are six sets of two values to be processed. When the READ statement is executed
for the first time, the program obtains the
values 5 and 9. The value 5 is assigned to
P and the value 9 is assigned to R. The program processes these values then replaces P
and R with 17 and 8. This procedure continues
until P and R are assigned zeroes. The program then finds that P equals zero and processing stops.

A DATA statement may appear anywhere in a
program as long as it appears ahead of the
END statement. The program will work in
exactly the same way regardless of where the
DATA statement is located.

What would you suppose?

May you have more than one DATA statement in
a program?

304   Yes, since one DATA statement may not
      be sufficient to supply all the required
      values.

305   No, one DATA statement is always enough.

FRAME 303

No, the program does not process seven sets.
Actually the program processes six. Examine
the DATA statement. You'll see that the first
six sets of values are actually processed.
The 7th set merely provides zeroes to P and
R. When P's value is found to be zero, the
program stops.

Please proceed to Frame 302.

FRAME 304

The answer is Yes, since one DATA statement
may not be sufficient to supply all the required values.

A person may place as many DATA statements
in a program as he pleases. These may be
placed at the beginning, near the end or
scattered throughout the program.

The program shown in Frame 300 would work
just as well if written this way:

```
10000    DATA 5, 9, 17
10050    DATA 8, 2, 16, 7, 13
10100    READ P, R
10200    IF P = 0 THEN 10500
10250    DATA 1, 44
10300    PRINT P, R, P * R
10400    GO TO 10100
10450    DATA 6, 7, 0, 0
10500    END
```

Do all these DATA statements act the same
as if all the values had been placed in one
DATA statement?

306 Yes

307 No, because only one DATA statement
     is permitted per program.

FRAME 305

No, your response indicates that you really don't understand why DATA and READ statements are used in programs. You should review the use of DATA and READ statements.

Please return to Frame 299 and proceed forward again from that point.

FRAME 306

The answer is definitely Yes.

In the interests of neatness, place all
DATA statements in one section of the program. This practice will help avoid con-
fusion when the values have to be changed.

Study this program:

```
10   DATA 8, 7, 9, 4, 5, 11, 14
20   READ J
30   PRINT J, J↑2, J↑3
40   GO TO 20
50   END
```

What will the program print on each line of
output?

308   The values of J, J squared, and J cubed.

309   The sum of J, J squared, and J cubed.

310   The largest of the three values J, J
squared, or J cubed.

FRAME 307

No, your answer is incorrect. Frame 304 says
that you may have more than one DATA statement
in your program. The example in the frame
shows that a program will work just as well
if you have several DATA statements scattered
in a program as it would if the DATA statement
was placed at one location. The computer has
no trouble finding all DATA statements.

Please proceed directly to Frame 306.

FRAME 308

The program will print the values of J, J squared, and J cubed.

How many lines of output will the program give?

311 7 cubed or 343

312 7

FRAME 309

No, the computer will not print the sum of J, J squared, and J cubed. The values of J, J squared, and J cubed will be printed. Those values will be printed in the first three zones of the output paper.

Please proceed directly to Frame 308.

FRAME 310

No, the computer will not print the largest of the three values J, J squared, and J cubed. The computer will merely print the actual values of J, J squared, and J cubed. The values of J used are, of course, 8, 7, 9, 4, 5, 11, and 14.

Please proceed directly to Frame 308.

FRAME 311

No, your answer is incorrect. The computer
will print 7 values, because there are 7 values
in the DATA statement. These 7 values: 8;
7; 9; 4; 5; 11; and 14 are obtained one at a
time by the READ statement. Please return
to Frame 299 to review this material. Then
proceed from that point.

FRAME 312

Yes, you're right. The program will print
7 lines of output. Then the program will
stop since it runs out of values to work
with. The program will print the message
OUT OF DATA, then stop.

Does the example program have an endless
loop?

313   Yes, because there's no way to get to
the END statement.

314   No, because the program automatically
stops when it runs out of data values.

FRAME 313

No, while there may appear to be an endless
loop in the program, there really is not.
The program goes to the READ statement several
times to obtain values. When the values run
out, the program stops.

Please go directly to Frame 314.

FRAME 314

The answer is No. When the program runs out
of data values to work with, it automatically
stops.

Suppose a teacher wants to compute the average
final grade in a class of ten students. The
DATA statement contains the ten grades to be
averaged. Study this program:

```
10   DATA 85, 66, 94, 83, 76, 71, 68, 83, 77, 98
20   LET T = 0
30   LET C = 0
40   READ M
50   LET T = T + M
60   LET C = C + 1
70   GO TO 40
80   PRINT T/C
90   END
```

Does this program accomplish the objective?

315   Yes, T/C is definitely the average grade.
      It is printed at line 80.

316   No, the program prints OUT OF DATA
      before the average grade is computed.

317   No, because average is really C/T.

FRAME 315

Your answer is reasonable, but it is incorrect.
It's true that T/C (total divided by count)
yields an average. The problem is that the
program never goes to line 80. When the GO
TO at line 70 directs the computer to go to
the READ statement for the eleventh time, the
program does not find an eleventh value and
therefore stops.

Please return to Frame 314 and make another
selection.

FRAME 316

Correct! The answer is No. The program prints OUT OF DATA before the average grade is computed.

This program correctly initializes a memory cell in which the total sum of grades is to be stored. The name of the cell is T and is given an initial value of zero. The program also initializes a cell to receive the count of values. The name of the cell is C and begins with an initial value of zero.

Every time a value is added to T, 1 is added to C. Unfortunately, the program never gets to line 80. The program runs out of data and the OUT OF DATA message is printed.

How can this difficulty be overcome?

318   A sentinel value may be placed at the end of the DATA statement. This value may be detected by an IF statement.

319   The program has to be rewritten so that it uses INPUT instead of READ and DATA.

320   Nothing can be done. It's impossible to obtain the average.

FRAME 317

No, the average is indeed T/C. In the program T means total of scores and C means count of scores.

Please return to Frame 314 and make a better selection.

FRAME 318

You're right.

The correct answer involves a sentinel value. A sentinel value may be placed at the end of the DATA statement. This value may be detected by an IF statement. To illustrate, here is a way that the program may be written:

```
10   DATA 85,66,94,83,76,71,68,83,77,98,1000
20   LET T = 0
30   LET C = 0
40   READ M
50   LET T = T + M
60   LET C = C + 1
70   GO TO 40
80   PRINT T/C
90   END
```

The sentinel value is 1000. It's safe to assume that a student's final grade cannot be 1000. Therefore, when the program detects this value it knows that all of the information has been accumulated and the average may be computed and printed.

How should a sentinel value, to be placed at the end of a DATA statement, be chosen?

321 It should always be zero or 1000.

322 It should be a value which has absolutely no chance of being an actual value to be processed.

323 Any number may be selected since the chances of the sentinel's value being confused with a real data value are remote.

FRAME 319

No, the INPUT statement does not help solve the problem. The problem will have no way to reach line 80. The program must detect when it has reached the end of the data.

Please return to Frame 316 and make a better selection.

FRAME 320

No, by now you should have a fairly good
feeling of what can and what can not be
done. It certainly is possible to obtain
the average of a series of numbers in a
DATA statement. What's really needed is a
way for the program to detect the end of
the numbers in the DATA statement.

Please return to Frame 316 and make a better
selection.

FRAME 321

No, the value does not always have to be zero
or 1000. The sentinel value should be one
that has absolutely no chance of being an
actual value in a DATA statement. If the
values were pay rates, then the sentinel value
could be -5, for example. If the values were
hours worked last week, the sentinel value
could be 500.

Please return to Frame 318 and make a better
selection.

FRAME 322

You're right!

A sentinel value should be a value that has absolutely no chance of being an actual value to be processed.

Placing a sentinel value at the end of a DATA statement permits the DATA statement to contain as many values as needed to solve a given problem. The example program could have either more or less than 10 values in the DATA statement. The program will work equally well.

The same program could be written using FOR and NEXT statements. This way:

```
10   DATA 85,66,94,83,76,71,68,83,77,98,1000
20   LET T = 0
40   FOR Z = 1 TO 50
50   READ M
60   IF M = 1000 THEN 100
70   LET T = T + M
90   NEXT Z
100  PRINT T/(Z-1)
110  END
```

No response required for this frame. Please go directly to Frame 324.

FRAME 323

No, to permit any number to be a sentinel
value is too risky. Suppose, for example,
that winter temperatures in Chicago were being
averaged. Since zero is a possible value,
then zero should not be used as a sentinel
value.

Please return to Frame 318 and give a better
response.

FRAME 324

This program has been set up to read a maximum of 50 grades. Less than 50 may be used
if a sentinel value is placed at the end of
the DATA statement.

The counter in the FOR statement, Z, counts
the number of grades which have been processed. When the sentinel is found, the
value of Z is one unit larger than it should
be, because the sentinel value was counted.
That's why 1 is subtracted from Z at line
100, where the average grade is computed.

Will the program give the correct answer if
exactly 50 grades are processed?

325   Yes, because the average mark is
      calculated immediately following
      the NEXT statement.

326   No, because the sentinel will never
      be detected.

327   No, because the count should be 50
      when the average is computed, but the
      program reduces it to 49.

FRAME 325

The answer is Yes, because the average mark
is calculated immediately following the NEXT
statement.

When 50 marks are processed, no sentinel is,
of course, necessary. The value of the counter
Z has nevertheless attained the value 51.
It should be reduced to 50. At line 100, the
value of Z is reduced by 1 and the average
value is correctly computed.

There is no response required for this frame.
Congratulations on successfully completing
Section VI.

Before going on to Section VII, please read
the special section on Flowcharting that
follows.

FRAME 326

Sorry, your response is incorrect. The program will process the 50th value, then increase Z by 1. Z's value will become 51. Since Z's value is now larger than 50, the program goes to line 100 and escapes from the FOR/NEXT loop.

The program will then compute the correct average (Z's value is reduced by 1, making it 50) and will print it.

Please proceed now to Frame 325.

FRAME 327

You're not exactly right. When the 50th value has been processed, the program does not escape from the loop immediately. Z is raised to 51, then escapes. When the average is computed at line 100, the program reduces Z's value to 50. The program therefore computes the correct average.

Please proceed directly to Frame 325.

SPECIAL SECTION

FLOWCHARTING

Before continuing your study of BASIC, you should become acquainted with the art of flowcharting. Up to this point, you have probably had little difficulty in telling the computer what you want done - the problems have been relatively simple. But now the problems will become more difficult and an introduction to flowcharting can be delayed no longer.

What is flowcharting? What is a flowchart?

A flowchart is a pictorial representation of what you want the computer to do. The process of developing the flowchart is called flowcharting.

A flowchart is shown on page 329.

To understand the flowchart, begin at the oval labeled BEGIN and follow the arrows. The flowchart indicates that zeroes are to be assigned to T and N. The BASIC statements accomplishing these objectives are:

            LET T = 0
            LET N = 0

Then, the flowchart indicates that a value V is to be obtained (read) from a DATA state-

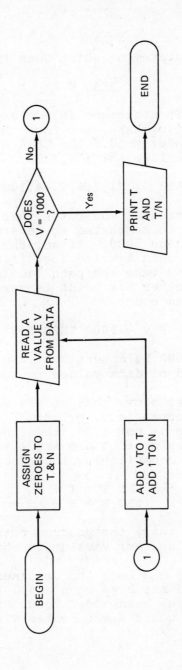

329

ment. The statement which does this is

READ V

Though a DATA statement is not explicitly
shown in a flowchart, the fact that one
exists is understood. The DATA statement
might be one like this:

DATA 8,21,7,6,9,-4,1000

The flowchart next indicates that the value
read, V, is to be tested to determine whether
it is the value 1000. If so, the program is
to take the path labeled Yes; if not, the
program is to take the path labeled NO. The
question whether V's value is zero is asked
by the IF statement

IF V = 1000 THEN 200

The value 1000 is a sentinel value, indica-
ting the end of data values to be processed.

The flowchart shows that if V's value is 1000,
then the program is to print a line of output;
if V's value is not 1000, then the program is
to add V's value to T and add 1 to N. The
statements accomplishing these actions are:

LET T = T + V
LET N = N + 1

Having done this, the program returns to the
point where another V value is obtained.

If V's value had been the sentinel value,
then V would not have been added to T and 1
would not have been added to N. Instead,
the program would have printed T and computed
and printed T/N.

As you may have already analyzed for yourself, this program sums a series of values found in the DATA statement and prints the sum (T) as well as the average (T/N) of the values. The variable, N, counts the number of data values read and added to T.

This is a program which might result from the flowchart above:

```
10   DATA 8, 21, 7, 6, 9, -4, 1000
20   LET T = 0
30   LET N = 0
40   READ V
50   IF V = 1000 THEN 200
60   LET T = T + V
70   LET N = N + 1
80   GO TO 40
200  PRINT T, T/N
210  END
```

You'll observe that the flowchart shows five differently shaped symbols. These symbols, along with their names, are:

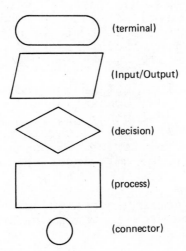

(terminal)

(Input/Output)

(decision)

(process)

(connector)

The terminal symbol is given at the beginning of a flowchart and at its end. The oval is placed in the upper lefthand corner of a page within the symbol, the words BEGIN, START, ENTER, or a word having a similar meaning are entered.

The I/O (input/output) symbol is used to indicate the reading of data from a DATA statement or the printing of answers. It is also used to indicate the usage of BASIC'S INPUT statement. The words normally found within the I/O parallelogram are READ, PRINT, WRITE, and INPUT.

The decision diamond is used to indicate a question being asked. The symbol indicates the usage of an IF statement. At least two arrows must exit from a decision diamond. These are often, but not always, labeled YES and NO.

The process symbol is used to indicate an assignment of values. Within the rectangle, the words "assign," "set," "compute," and others are used. These words indicate that the LET statement is to be used to assign a value (LET T = 0) or to compute a value (LET N = N + 1).

The connector symbol is used to shorten lines within a flowchart or to continue a flowchart upon another page. Any desired character may be placed within the connector circle. A line is assumed to exist between two connector symbols inscribed with the same character.

Arrows connecting these various symbols show the sequence in which the instructions are to be executed.

Suppose we have 30 quiz scores in a DATA
statement that we would like to sum and compute the average. The flowchart of a program to accomplish the task is: (as shown on
page 334).

The program is this:

```
 10   LET S = 0
 20   LET C = 1
 30   IF C > 30 THEN 80
 40   READ V
 50   LET S = S + V
 60   LET C = C + 1
 70   GO TO 30
 80   PRINT S/30
 90   DATA 73, 85, 76, 93, 99, 85, 63, 67, 75, 76
100   DATA 43, 90, 88, 78, 77, 58, 93, 87, 85, 73
110   DATA 74, 84, 77, 92, 100, 84, 62, 86, 87, 72
120   END
```

S is used to sum the values; C to count the
values so that it will be known when 30 values
have been processed.

Suppose it is not known exactly how many data
values are in the DATA statement to be processed.
A sentinel value may be placed at the end of the
DATA. Then the program can search for it as it
processes valid quiz scores. Let us assume the
sentinel value is 1000. This is the flowchart
we can use: (as shown on page 335).

The program is:

```
 10   LET S = 0
 20   LET C = 0
 30   READ V
 40   IF V = 1000 THEN 80
 50   LET S = S + V
 60   LET C = C + 1
```
(continued on page 336.)

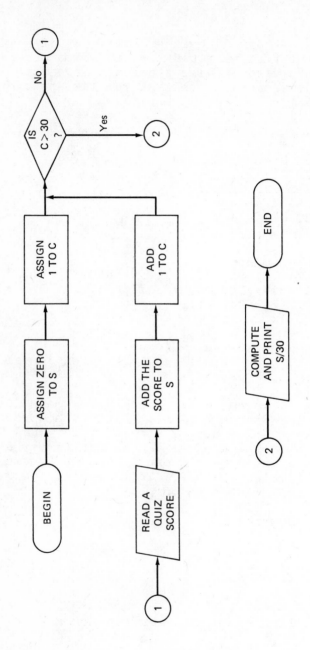

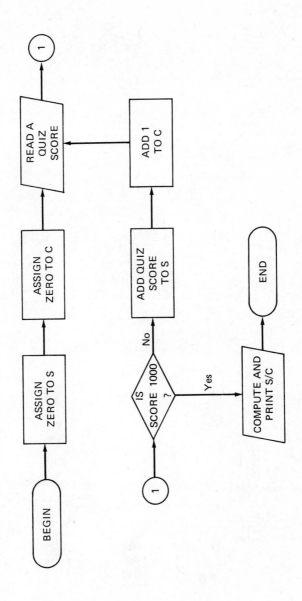

335

```
70    GO TO 30
80    PRINT S/C
90    DATA 75, 82, 76, 95, 32, 83, 91, 83
100   DATA 1000
110   END
```

SECTION VII

ARRAYS

FRAME 328

There are times when your program will have to transfer information from the DATA statement to a special working area especially set up to process the information. The special working area is set up using a DIM statement.

Example:

```
100   DIM Q (15)
110   DATA 18,9,7,6,4,6,3,16,81,42,9,56,17,6,2
120   FOR A = 1 TO 15
130   READ Q (A)
140   NEXT A
        ⋮  ⎫
        ⋮  ⎬  Additional Program Statements
        ⋮  ⎭
```

This program sets up a working area in memory which has a size of 15 memory positions. See line 100. That working area has a name. Can you tell what it is?

329   DIM

330   Q

FRAME 329

No, your answer is not correct. Look at line 100. The statement is:

$$100 \quad DIM \quad Q(15)$$

The word DIM is an abbreviation for dimension. A working area is being set aside. The name of that area is Q and size is 15. In the working space 15 memory cells are being set aside.

Please proceed to Frame 330.

FRAME 330

The name of the working area is Q. (The
name of a working area must always consist
of a single letter of the alphabet.) Q consists of 15 memory cells. Those memory cells
look like this:

WORKING AREA Q

0	0	0	0	0	0	0	0	0	0	0	0	0	0	0
1	2	3	4	5	6	7	8	9	10	11	12	13	14	15

What is the value which is initially given
to each of these 15 memory cells?

331   Zero

332   Blanks

FRAME 331

The values initially given to the cells
are zeroes.

The numbers shown under the 15 cells are
labels which identify the cells. The first
cell is cell 1; the second cell is 2; and
the last is cell 15.

Where is cell 16?

333   There is none.

334   It follows cell 15.

335   Since it's not shown, cell 16 could
      be anywhere.

FRAME 332

No, if you'll examine the illustration in Frame 330, you'll see that each square representing a memory cell has the value zero in it. We can conclude that zeroes are the initial values assigned to a working area.

Please proceed now to Frame 331.

FRAME 333

There is no cell 16, because the DIM statement calls for only 15 cells to be set aside.
If the DIM statement had been written this
way

100   DIM Q (100)

then the number of cells set aside in working area Q would have been 100. If this
DIM statement had been used, where would
cell 16 be?

336   Immediately following cell 15.

337   There is none - you can't have a
      working area containing more than
      15 cells.

FRAME 334

No, your answer is incorrect. Examine Frame 330 again and you'll see that there are 15 squares. The 15 squares were defined by the DIM statement which read

$$100 \quad DIM \quad Q(15)$$

If the number within parentheses were larger, there would be a cell 16. As of now, there is none.

Please proceed to Frame 333.

FRAME 335

No, your answer isn't a good one. Look
again at Frame 330. Only 15 squares are
shown in the illustration. The 15 cells
were set up by the statement reading:

$$100 \quad DIM \ Q(15)$$

If more than 15 cells had been wanted, the
number within parentheses would have been
larger. Then there would have been a cell
16. As of now, there is none.

Please go to Frame 333.

FRAME 336

Yes, you're right!

Cell 16 would be located immediately following cell 15. When you set up a special working area, you may give it any name you please and you may give it any size you please up to 1023 computer cells.

Here is the way some DIM's may be set up:

```
400   DIM B(40)
410   DIM C(100), D(75)
```

How many working areas are shown in the above two statements?

338   Two

339   Three

340   215

FRAME 337

No, you've missed the point. There definitely is a cell 16, if the DIM statement
reads

$$100 \quad DIM \ Q(100)$$

The best plan for you at this point is to
return to Frame 328 and proceed from there.
Please do so and take your time.

FRAME 338

No, while there are two DIM statements in the program, one defines two working areas.

Please return to Frame 336 and count the working areas again.

FRAME 339

You're right.

Three is the correct answer.
The names of the three working areas are
B, C, and D. The sizes of the working
areas are 40, 100, and 75, respectively.
Consider the first working area, B, which
has a size of 40 cells.

Each cell has its own identifying position
number. Thus, the first B cell is labeled
B_1, the second B_2, etc. The last is B_{40}.

Do we know if there is a memory cell called
B_{30}?

341 Yes

342 No

343 We don't have enough facts to answer
     this question.

FRAME 340

No, you've confused the size of the working areas with the number of working areas. The combined size of the working areas is 215. But how many working areas are there?

Please return to Frame 336 and count them again.

FRAME 341

Yes, there is.

The answer is Yes, because all three working areas were set up with at least 30
memory cells. You can see, though, that
there may not be a cell labeled B_{80}. Nor
may there be a D_{80}. A cell identified as
C_{80} is valid.

The small figures shown to the right and
slightly below the names of the working
space names are called "subscripts."

What does the subscript do?

344 The subscript tells the maximum size
   of a working area.

345 The subscript points to a specific
   memory cell in a specific working
   area.

346 The subscript causes a zero to be
   placed in the specific memory cell
   identified by the subscript.

FRAME 342

Your answer is not correct. Examine the DIM statement in lines 400 and 410:

$$400 \quad DIM \ B(49)$$
$$410 \quad DIM \ C(100), \ D(75)$$

Observe that there is a 40th cell for each of the working areas B, C, and D. The 40 B cells extend from B_1 through B_{40}; the 100 C cells extend from C_1 through C_{100}; and the 75 D cells extend from D_1 through D_{75}.

Please proceed now to Frame 341.

FRAME 343

Your answer is not at all correct. You do have enough information to answer the question. Please proceed to Frame 342 for more information, then proceed to Frame 341.

FRAME 344

No, a subscript doesn't tell what the maximum size of a working area is. That information is given in a DIM statement. Actually, a subscript tells <u>which</u> one memory cell is being referred to. When we mention B_{30}, we are referring to the 30th cell in working area B. The maximum size of B is given in the DIM statement

$$400 \quad DIM \ B(40)$$

Please go to Frame 345.

FRAME 345

A subscript points to a specific memory cell in a specific working area.

To have your program move several values from a DATA statement to a working area, you may effectively use a FOR/NEXT loop. Here's a model of how the task may be accomplished.

```
100   DIM  Q(15)
110   DATA 18,9,7,6,4,6,3,16,81,42,9,56,17,6,2
120   FOR A = 1 TO 15
130   READ Q(A)
140   NEXT A
      ⋮  }  Additional Program Statements
```

This is only the first part of a program. The dotted lines below statement 140 indicate that more statements are in the program.

Have you seen these five statements before?

347   Yes, at the beginning of this section.

348   They look a little familiar, but I can't place them.

FRAME 346

No, this response has no relationship to what
has been said so far. Somewhere along the
line, you've gotten off the track.

Please return to Frame 328 and resume from
that point. Go slowly this time.

FRAME 347

Yes, at the beginning of this section.

Now that we've had a brief introduction to
working areas, we can explore in more detail the statements shown at the beginning
of the section.

The statement reading

100   DIM Q(15)

sets up a working space named Q. The working space contains 15 memory cells. The
initial values assigned to those memory
cells are zeroes.

Observe that the DATA statement at line
110 contains 15 actual values. What would
you guess the program is going to do with
those values?

349   They will be deleted since they are
       unneeded.

350   They will be transferred to the
       working area called Q.

FRAME 348

You couldn't have studied Frame 328 very carefully. Please review Frame 328, then proceed directly to Frame 345.

FRAME 349

No, your answer is not realistic. The 15
numbers are to be used. Please read Frame
347 to determine why your answer should be
changed. Then make another selection.

FRAME 350

You're right! The values will be transferred to the working area called Q.

In order to transfer the values, the READ statement is employed. Observe that the READ statement in the body of the loop is controlled by FOR and NEXT statements. How many times will the loop be executed?

351 As often as required to transfer values from the DATA statement to the working space. The actual number of times is a variable and is unknown at this time.

352 Once.

353 Fifteen times.

FRAME 351

Your answer is not correct. The actual number of times is known since other facts are known. For example, the DIM statement for the Q working area has set aside 15 memory cells. Also, it is known that there are 15 values in the DATA statement and that all of them must be moved to the working area.

Please return to Frame 350 and make a better selection.

361

FRAME 352

Sorry, your answer is not right. The loop
will have to be executed several more times
than once. After all, there are 15 values
in the DATA statement which must be moved to
the working area Q. Does this give you a
hint?

Please return to Frame 350 and make a better
selection.

FRAME 353

Right!   The answer is 15 times.

You'll recall that the FOR/NEXT loop looks
like this

```
120   FOR A = 1 TO 15
130   READ Q(A)
140   NEXT A
```

The counter which controls this loop is A.
A will have the values 1, 2, 3,..., 15 as
the loop cycles from statement 120 through
140.

Is A also used as a subscript?

354   Yes, in statement 130.

355   No, a counter cannot also be a sub-
      script.

FRAME 354

Yes, in statement 130.

In statement 130, we see this statement:

130   READ Q(A)

A READ statement obtains a value from a DATA statement and assigns it to the variable named-in this case Q. But which Q? The value of A tells which Q is involved. What is the value of A when the loop is executed for the first time?

356   1

357   18

FRAME 355

Your answer is not correct.

Do you recall what a subscript is? A subscript is a number, name, or expression
which references a particular entry of a
working space. In BASIC the subscript is
in parentheses. A is definitely used as
a subscript in this frame since, at different times, it references 15 elements
in the Q working area.

Please proceed to Frame 354.

FRAME 356

You are correct!

The value of A is 1. Since A is shown as the subscript for the working area named Q, the subscript tells us that the value read from the DATA statement is to be assigned to the first Q memory cell. This means that the value 18 (the first value in the DATA statement) is to be assigned to Q_1.

The loop is then repeated. What value does Q_2 receive?

358   2

359   9

FRAME 357

Your answer is incorrect and appears to be
guesswork. When the loop is executed for
the first time the value of A is 1; when
executed for the second time, the value of
A is 2; etc. The correct answer to the
question is, therefore, 1.

You should return to Frame 328 now to review the FOR/NEXT statements, DIM's, and
subscripts. Please do so and resume moving
forward at that point.

FRAME 358

No, you must not confuse a subscript with the content of the referenced memory cell.

When we speak of Q_2, we're referring to the second memory cell of the working space Q. The number 2 is the subscript, but the second value in the DATA statement is 9. This is the value which is assigned to Q_2.

Please proceed now to Frame 359.

FRAME 359

The answer is 9.

The value 9 is obtained from the DATA statement and assigned to Q_2. The READ statement shows the subscript A.

$$130 \quad READ \ Q(A)$$

Since A contains the value 2 during the
second time that the loop is executed. A
references the second Q memory cell. That
cell receives the second value from the
DATA statement, which is 9.

Does the FOR/NEXT loop transfer all 15
values from the DATA statement to the
working area named Q?

360 Yes

361 All except the last one.

FRAME 360

The answer is Yes.

After the 15 values have been moved to working space Q, the working space has these values stored in the cells:

WORKING AREA Q

18	9	7	6	4	6	3	16	81	42	9	56	17	6	2

The original zero values in those 15 cells have been replaced by the values shown.

The working area now contains an array of numbers. An array is a group of related numbers arranged in some meaningful order.

What is the seventh value of the Q array?

362   3

363   81

FRAME 361

No, your answer is not right. Examine the
program carefully. The loop is executed
15 times; the subscript A varies from 1
through 15 in steps of 1; and that 15
values are obtained from the DATA statement. The simple answer to the question
is Yes.

Please proceed to Frame 360.

FRAME 362

The answer is 3.

The value 3 is found in the seventh memory cell in the array named Q. Therefore, Q_7 contains that value.

Suppose the statement at line 150 of the program reads like this:

150   PRINT Q(14)

What value will the program print?

364   6

365   14

FRAME 363

No, not quite. In order to ascertain the
answer to the question you must count
(from left to right) to the seventh square
in the array. The seventh square contains
the value 3. This number gives the answer
to the question.

The value 81 isn't the correct answer,
since Q_9 not Q_7 holds that value. Similarly, the value 18 isn't right, since
Q_1 holds that value, not Q_7.

Please proceed to Frame 362.

FRAME 364

The answer is 6.

The number 14 is a subscript. It indicates
that the value to be printed is the 14th
value of the Q array. The 14th value of the
array is 6. The printer therefore prints 6.

Subscripts may be actual numbers, variable
names, or expressions. These subscripts
might be found at statements 500, 510, and
520 of the program shown in Frame 328.

```
500   PRINT Q(5)
510   PRINT Q(P)
520   PRINT Q((D + E)/F)
```

Do you agree that the above statements are
OK?

366   Yes, assuming variables P, D, E and
      F have previously been assigned values.

367   No, because subscripts used must show
      the variable name A, not P, D, E or F.

FRAME 365

No, you appear to be confusing the content
of an array location with a subscript.
The line number of the PRINT statement is
150; the subscript value is 14. At the
14th location of the Q array the value 6
is found.

The correct answer to the question is,
therefore, 6. Please proceed now to Frame
364.

FRAME 366

The answer is Yes, assuming variables P, D,
E, and F have previously been assigned values.

Subscripts may be actual numbers, variable
names, and/or expressions. The computed subscripts must always be whole numbers and they
may never be less than 1 or larger than the
maximum size of the array named.

Is the subscript in this statement OK?

600   PRINT Q(19)

368   No, because the maximum size of Q is 15.

369   Yes, the program will enlarge Q as
        needed.

FRAME 367

Your answer is not right. The variable
name A is not only the name which may be
used as a subscript for Q. The array Q
can be referenced by any legal subscript
at any time in a program. Sometimes the
subscript is A; sometimes an actual number
like 5; sometimes a variable name like P,
Q, or R; sometimes an expression like I +
K, (F + G)/R, or (A * L)/(E - W).

Please proceed to Frame 366.

FRAME 368

The answer is No.

A subscript may be: an actual number, such as 12; a variable name, such as D; or an expression such as (P + R) * T. When a variable name is used as a subscript, a value must have been assigned to the name at some point earlier in the program. Any computed subscript must be an integer and must be within the required range.

There is no response for this frame. Please go to Frame 370.

FRAME 369

No, your answer is not well thought out.
You know that the DIM statement for Q gives
a size of 15. This means that the largest
A subscript may be 15. The computer has
no way to enlarge Q.

The simple fact is that Q(19) has no meaning and is therefore incorrect.

Please go to Frame 368 now.

FRAME 370

If a variable name or an expression gives a value which is not a whole number, the program will drop the fractional portion of the value and use the whole number portion as the subscript. Thus, if the subscript value appears to be 12.3, the program will use 12. If the value appears to be 9.8, the program will use 9.

Here are some examples of legal subscripts used in expressions:

```
50   LET P(3) = 62.77
60   LET P(K) = 2.1
70   LET P(N * 3 + L * 2) = 14.8
```

What is the name of the array being mentioned in these examples?

371   P

372   K

FRAME 371

Yes, the name of the array is P.

In this example, the variable P is the name of an array. This array is defined in a DIM statement near the beginning of the program. The DIM statement also gives P's size. Example:

$$5 \quad DIM \quad P(500)$$

If an erroneous subscript is ever computed and an attempt is made to use it, the system will type a message telling you that a subscript error has been made; the system will then stop. If a statement is:

$$70 \quad LET \ P(N * 3 + L * 2) = 12.8$$

and N holds the value 50 while L holds the value 100, will the program accept the subscript for P? Assume that the DIM statement is as shown above.

373   Yes.

374   No.

FRAME 372

No, your answer is not right. Keep in mind
that the subscript is shown within parentheses to the right of the variable being
referenced. In line 50, the subscript is 3;
in line 60, it is K; and in line 70, it is
N * 3 + L * 2

Does this additional information concerning
what a subscript is help you give a better
answer to the question? Please return to
Frame 370 and select another, better response.

FRAME 373

Yes. The subscript is legal. Its value
is 350 (50 * 3 + 100 * 2). The P array
permits a maximum subscript of 500. After
an array has been established you will
probably want to have your program do
something with it. Values in an array may
be summed, searched, sorted, or processed
in many other ways. Suppose we want to
have 15 values in an array summed and an
average computed. May subscripts be used
to help accomplish this task? What would
you guess?

375   Yes, that's the topic under dis-
      cussion in this section.

376   No, an array will definitely be
      required, but it's easier not to
      use subscripts for this problem.

FRAME 374

Sorry, your answer is incorrect. The subscript N * 3 + L * 2 is acceptable since it
reduces to 50 * 3 + 100 * 2 which equals 350.
The working area P has been established with
a size of 500. The subscript is therefore
OK.

It's possible, of course for N and L to hold
values other than 50 and 100. In this case,
the subscript might be wrong. We'd have to
know the values of N and L in order to make
a determination.

Please proceed to Frame 373.

FRAME 375

Yes, that's the topic under discussion in this section.

Here is a portion of the program which sums values in an array and computes an average. Assume that there are 15 values in the array - those values having been transferred from a DATA statement.

```
100   DIM Q(15)
         ⋮    ⎫    Additional Program Statements
              ⎭
200   S = 0
210   FOR W = 1 TO 15
220   LET S = S + Q(W)
230   NEXT W
240   PRINT S/15
250   END
```

In this example what is the name of the array?

377   Q

378   W

FRAME 376

Sorry, your reply is not correct. We know
we asked you to make a guess, but if you had
understood all the material given so far, you
should have been able to give a better answer.

Please return to Frame 328 to review arrays,
subscripts, loops, etc. Then proceed from
that point.

FRAME 377

Yes, the name of the array is Q.

We can see that this is true, because the
subscript W is used with the variable name
Q. Also a DIM statement appears mentioning
Q. Whenever the name of an array is shown
in a program, a subscript must always follow it. The variable names S and W are
not array names. They are the names for
a single cell in the memory of the computer.

What does the statement

$$220 \quad \text{LET } S = S + Q(W)$$

do?

379   It causes the average of 15 array
       values to be computed.

380   It causes a value of Q to be added
       to S, thereby obtaining an updated S.

381   It exchanges the values found in S
       with the 15 values found in the
       array Q.

FRAME 378

No, that is not the name of the array. A way
to check for an array name is to see whether
a DIM statement exists for the array. Also,
is there a subscript given in connection with
a name? In this example, the DIM statement
at line 100 and the assignment statement at
line 220 should give useful clues.

Please return to Frame 375 and make another
selection.

FRAME 379

No, the statement does not cause averaging
in any way. Observe that the value Q(W)
is added to S and the result is placed
back in S. The values of W can, of course,
be any value from 1 through 15.

Please return to Frame 377 and make a
better selection.

FRAME 380

The statement causes a value of Q to be added
to S thereby updating S.

You can see that W is the name of a variable
which takes the place of subscripts 1, 2, 3,
4, etc., all the way through 15. The loop,
bounded by line numbers 210 through 230, is
executed 15 times. Each time it is executed,
W takes on a different value. It is the same
as if the program had been written this way:

```
100   DIM Q(15)
         :  ⎫
         :  ⎬    Additional Program Statements
         :  ⎭
200   LET S = 0
210   LET S = S + Q(1)
220   LET S = S + Q(2)
230   LET S = S + Q(3)

         :  ⎫
         :  ⎬    Additional Program Statements
         :  ⎭
350   LET S = S + Q(15)
360   PRINT S/15
370   END
```

Does the above program solve the given problem
just as well as the one which uses a FOR/NEXT
loop?

382   Yes, but it requires more statements.

383   Yes, but the program runs much slower.

FRAME 381

No, the statement does not exchange anything. Actually it adds the value Q(W)
to S, thereby updating S. The value of
W can be any number between 1 and 15 inclusive.

Please return to Frame 377 and make a
better selection.

FRAME 382

Yes, but it requires more statements.

A program which uses a FOR/NEXT loop in deal-
ing with an array is invariably much shorter
than one which gives every array element as
a separate item. Imagine how many statements
would be required if the array had 1000 separate values!

No response required for this frame.

Congratulations on having completed Section
VII.

FRAME 383

Sorry, you're wrong. The program does give exactly the same answers. The program runs as fast as if FOR/NEXT had been used. The main difference is that more statements are needed. Consider this example:

```
10   FOR J = 1,10        10  PRINT  "HELLO"
20   PRINT "HELLO"       20  PRINT  "HELLO"
30   NEXT J              30  PRINT  "HELLO"
40   END                 40  PRINT  "HELLO"
                         50  PRINT  "HELLO"
                         60  PRINT  "HELLO"
                         70  PRINT  "HELLO"
                         80  PRINT  "HELLO"
                         90  PRINT  "HELLO"
                         100 PRINT  "HELLO"
                         110 END
```

The side-by-side programs accomplish the same result-to print HELLO 10 times.
Please go to Frame 382.

SECTION VIII

USING ARRAYS

FRAME 384

At times an array will have to be searched for a particular value. Here is a program that searches an array named V for the smallest value.

```
100   DIM V(500)
         ⋮  ⎫
         ⋮  ⎬   Additional Program Statements
         ⋮  ⎭
200   LET S = V(1)
210   FOR T = 2 TO 500
220   IF S <= V(T) THEN 240
230   LET S = V(T)
240   NEXT T
250   PRINT S
260   END
```

What is being done in statements which are not shown?

385   The sum of the values in the V array is being computed.

386   Data values are being transferred to array V from DATA statements.

387   The array is being searched for the number 240.

FRAME 385

No, the sum of the values in the V array is not being computed. Frame 384 tells what the program does. Please return to Frame 384, read it carefully, then give another response to the question.

FRAME 386

Data values are being transferred to the array V from DATA statements. This has to be the best answer because nothing can be done with an array until values are loaded into it. it.

At line 200 the <u>first</u> value of the V array is placed in S. S stands for "smallest value." At line 200, therefore, S is initialized to hold the first value of the V array. (200 LET S = V(1)). Why is this being done?

388 Because it is known that the first location of the V array holds the smallest value.

389 Because S needs a starting value. Other values in the V array will later have a chance to take V(1)'s place.

390 There is no good reason for doing this. It's just something programmers do.

FRAME 387

No, the program is not searching for the value 240. Look at the IF statement at line 220. There's a good clue there. Please read Frame 384 again and make another response.

FRAME 388

No, it is not known that the first value of
the V array is where you will find the smallest value. The whole point of the routine
is to determine <u>which</u> value is smallest.
In doing so, the first value of the V array
is placed in the memory cell named S.

Please return to Frame 386 read it again,
and make another selection.

FRAME 389

Correct.
Because S needs a starting value. Other
values in the V array will later have a
chance to take V(1)'s place.

The program cycles through the other 499
values of the V array, from V(2) through
V(500). Whenever the program finds a
value which is smaller than S, the program replaces S's value with the smaller
one.

In what line is S's value replaced with
a new V value?

391 220

392 230

FRAME 390

No, programmers don't like to give a computer
needless program steps. There is a definite
reason why the first value of the V array is
placed in the memory cell named S. Keep in
mind what the problem is - to find out which
value in the V array is smallest. It could
be any of the 500 values.

Please return to Frame 386 read it again and
make a better selection.

FRAME 391

No, your answer is not correct. Let's analyze the program steps. At line 200, the program gives S an initial value from V(1); at line 210, the program begins a loop which is intended to execute statements 220, 230, and 240, 499 times. The objective is to examine all memory cells from V(2) through V(500) to find values which are less than S.

The statement which actually tests a V value against S is the IF statement at line 220. If a V value being examined is actually smaller than S, that value is assigned to S at line 230; if not the program examines the next V value.

Please return to Frame 389 and make the correct selection.

FRAME 392

The line is 230.

At line 230, the statement

230   LET S = V (T)

causes a new V value to replace S. Which value actually replaces S depends on the value that T has. T is a subscript and cycles from 2 through 500. If V(1) contains the value 9.4, and V(2) contains the value 8.5, will S's value change?

393   Yes, because V(2)'s value is smaller than S's value.

394   No, because V(1)'s value was never stored in S.

395   Yes, because T's value is less than 9.4.

FRAME 393

You're right. The answer is Yes, because
V(2)'s value is smaller than S's value.
How many additional times, maximum, may
S's value change in this program?

396   Almost 500 times.

397   No, more than 3 times.

FRAME 394

Your answer is incorrect. V(1)'s value was
definitely stored in S. This happened at
line 200 of the program. Your understanding
of what is happening in this program seems a
little weak. Please return to Frame 384 to
begin fresh with the examples. Then proceed
from that point.

FRAME 395

Your answer is not right. T's value has
nothing to do with the relationship between
V(1) and V(2). The value in V(1) was assigned to S so that 5 holds the value 9.4.
If V(2)'s value is 8.5, then V(2)'s value
is less than S, which will definitely change.

Your understanding of this example seems
to be a little weak. Please return to
Frame 384 to begin the example again.
Then proceed.

FRAME 396

Almost 500 times.

S's value could change almost 500 more times, but it probably will not. S's value only changes when V(T) contains a value smaller than S. If the V values are thoroughly scrambled, S's value will change only 6 times or so. After the loop terminates, the program prints S. This will be the smallest of the 500 values in the array.

A program can be written to search an array for a particular value. How may that value be given to the program?

398   It may be entered via an INPUT statement.

399   It may be entered via an IF or PRINT statement.

FRAME 397

Your answer may be right, but is not as good as the answer which reads "almost 500 times." The point is that there is no way to tell how badly sequenced the V array is. If it is almost in increasing sequence, then S will not change very often. It could change only once, or as few as three times. But if the V array is badly scrambled, S could change several times. The worst case would be if the V array were in descending sequence, then every new value examined would be less than S. After its initial setting, S would change 499 times.

Please proceed to Frame 396.

FRAME 398

A value may be entered via an INPUT statement.
Study this example:

```
100    DATA 3,9,7,7,2,8,4,11,17,13,1,21,5,16,10
110    DIM W(15)
120    FOR B = 1 TO 15
130    READ W(B)
140    NEXT B
150    PRINT "TYPE IN A NUMBER TO SEARCH FOR"
160    INPUT V
170    FOR C = 1 to 15
180    IF W(C) = V THEN 220
190    NEXT C
200    PRINT "THAT NUMBER IS NOT IN THE ARRAY"
210    GO TO 230
220    PRINT "FOUND AT POSITION";C
230    END
```

There are two subscripts used in this program.
Name them.

```
400    W and V
401    B and C
```

FRAME 399

No, you seem to have forgotten some of the
BASIC you learned in the earlier sections.
Data values may certainly be entered by the
INPUT statement. Also, by the READ and LET
statements. Neither an IF statement, nor a
PRINT statement can introduce values into
the program. Recall that an IF statement
looks like this:

IF X = Y THEN 70

and a PRINT statement like this:

PRINT P/Q,S

These statements <u>test</u> values and <u>print</u> them,
but do not enter them.

Please go directly to Frame 398.

FRAME 400

No, your answer is not correct. This is disturbing. At this point in your study of BASIC, you should have no difficulty finding subscripts. Subscripts are always shown within parentheses. Thus, B and C are subscripts, because at lines 130 and 180 those names are shown within parentheses. The name W, and V are not shown within parentheses.

If at this point you feel unsure about subscripts, you should return to Frame 328 to make a new beginning on the subject. If you feel you can proceed, please go directly to Frame 401, but do not hesitate to return to Frame 328.

FRAME 401

The subscripts are B and C.

The two subscripts are used in two loops of
the W array. (It is all right to use several subscript names with one array.) Observe that the subscript you name in a FOR
statement will be initialized with the value
given in the FOR statement following the
word FOR. The first loop initializes B at
1 and increases B by 1 until it is greater
than 15. The second loop does the same with
the variable C. The two loops are indepen-
dent. First one is executed, then the other.

What is the name of the array in which the
value named V is searched for?

402 W

403 B

FRAME 402

The name of the array is W, and has a size
of 15 memory cells. Please examine the program in Frame 398, then answer this question:
When does a person type in a value for V?

404 The programmer interrupts the program
by hitting the BREAK key. Then he
types in a value for V.

405 The programmer does this when the
program reaches the END statement.

406 After the program reaches the INPUT
statement and types a question mark.

FRAME 403

The name you gave is not correct. Actually the name of the array is W. Observe that whenever the name W is given, a subscript always follows within parentheses. B and C are subscript names.

Please proceed directly to Frame 402.

FRAME 404

No, this sounds as if it would work, but it
will not. When you depress the BREAK key,
the program stops. If the program were to
be restarted, it would restart at the beginning of the program.

Please return to Frame 402 and make another
selection.

FRAME 405

No, this is not the correct method. When a program reaches the END statement, it simply stops. Any attempt to begin again always causes a restart from the first instruction.

Please return to Frame 402 and make another selection.

FRAME 406

Your answer is correct. This happens after the program reaches the INPUT statement and types a question mark on the terminal's output paper.

This program accepts only one V value from the terminal. It either finds the value in the array and types a message saying so or it does not find it and types another message giving the opposite comment. If this program were to search repeatedly for V values, what statements would you change and/or add in the program?

407   Statements 160 and 170 making them read:
                160 INPUT V AGAIN
                170 FOR C = 1 to V

408   Statements 180 and 185 making them read:
           180 IF W(C) = V(C) THEN 230
           185 NEXT W

409   Statements 230 and 240 making them read:
                230 GO TO 150
                240 END

FRAME 407

Your answer is not correct. This question called for a guess on your part, but it's really not an unfair question. If you have been following the text closely, you would be able to rule out two of the alternative responses. The remaining one would make sense and indeed be correct.

The first response can be ruled out because line 170 makes no sense at all. The counter in the loop would vary from 1 to whatever value was entered.

The second response can be ruled out because V is not an array, yet it has a subscript.

The third response has to be the correct one. Please go directly to Frame 409.

FRAME 408

Your answer is not correct. This question
called for a guess on your part, but it's
really not an unfair question. If you have
been following the text closely, you would
be able to rule out two of the alternative
responses. The remaining one would make
sense and indeed be correct.

The first response can be ruled out because
line 170 makes no sense at all. The counter
in the loop would vary from 1 to whatever
value was entered.

The second response can be ruled out because
V is not an array, yet it has a subscript.

The third response has to be the correct one.

Please go directly to Frame 409.

FRAME 409

The statements at line 230 and 240 should be changed to make them read:

        230   GO TO 150
        240   END

This program now cycles back to line 150 as many times as the programmer wants. When he wants the program to stop, the programmer may hit the BREAK key on the keyboard. The program will end immediately.

An alternative method of having the program stop is to place this statement in the program:

        165   IF V = 0 THEN 240

If this statement is in the program, when will the program stop?

410   When the user types a zero in response to the program's question mark.

411   When the programmer depresses the SHIFT key and the RETURN key simultaneously.

FRAME 410

The correct answer is "when the user types in a zero in response to the program's question mark."

It goes without saying that the program can be made to check for any input value the programmer wishes to give. He must select a value which he is certain does not appear as a legitimate value in the DATA statement.

In BASIC, arrays may have more than one specific size. Arrays may also be two dimensional. How would you guess a two dimensional array would be defined?

412   100   DIM M (45), M(20)

413   100   DIM (45,20)M

414   100   DIM M (45,20)

FRAME 411

No, the text does not say anything even remotely related to your response. If you place the statement

165 IF V = 0 THEN 240

following line 160 in the program, the program will check the value of V which is entered. If that value is zero, the program will jump to line 240 where the END statement is located. The program will then stop.

Please proceed now to Frame 410.

FRAME 412

No, your response

$$100 \quad DIM \ M(45), \ M(20)$$

makes it appear that your program uses two arrays, each called M, having different sizes.

Please return to Frame 410 and make another selection.

FRAME 413

No, you have the right idea, but made an incorrect selection. The name of an array always precedes its size.

Please return to Frame 410 and make another selection.

FRAME 414

Right!   The answer is

100   DIM M (45,20)

The working space established by this statement is organized with 45 rows and 20 columns.
There are 900 (45 x 20) memory cells in the
working space.   The name of the area is M.

In order to better visualize a two dimensional
area, consider one smaller than M.

200   DIM B (5,6)

How many memory cells are used in this working
area?

415   30

416   56

FRAME 415

The correct response is 30.

The name of the area is B and it is organized to have 5 rows and 6 columns. The 30 memory cells have been arranged this way:

We may transfer 30 data values from the DATA statement to B. There is a simple BASIC command which makes it easy to read these 30 values. Which of these statements would you say it is:

417   1000 MAT READ B

418   1000 FOR READ 1,5,1,6,B

FRAME 416

No, the very simple response is 30. Multiply
the number of rows (5) by the number of columns (6), and the answer is obtained. An illustration of the defined working space is
shown in Frame 415. Please go there now.

FRAME 417

1000 MAT READ B is correct.

The letters MAT stand for "matrix." The MAT READ command causes enough values to be read from the DATA statement to completely fill the working space defined by the DIM statement. Here is an example.

```
100    DIM B (5, 6)
110    DATA 3,8,9,7,2,4,15,0,6,0
120    DATA 1,8,1,3,8,9,3,1,0,12
130    DATA 13,10,16,4,8,4,0,8,12,3
140    MAT READ B
        ⋮
```

The MAT READ instructions will place the 30 values into the B area by rows. The first six values will be placed on the top row, the next six values on the second row, etc. When all values have been read, the result will be the array B.

How many rows does the DIM statement define for the B area?

419   6

420   5

FRAME 418

No, your answer is not correct. Frame 415
says that there is a simple BASIC command
enabling a program to read values into the
defined area. Your response does not look
simple. The simplest one given is

```
1000   MAT READ B
```

and is the correct one. Once the statement
has been executed, the program has obtained
30 values from the DATA statement and arranged
them to form an array of numbers. Another
word meaning array is matrix, which is where
the MAT in the command comes from.

Please go directly now to Frame 417.

FRAME 419

No, look at the DIM statement for B. It
reads

100 DIM B(5,6)

The first number given within parentheses is
the number that tells how many rows there are.
The second number tells how many columns.
To remind you which number stands for row
and which for column, you might remember Red
Cross. R, being the first letter, stands
for row and C, being the second letter,
stands for column.

Please go to Frame 420.

FRAME 420

There are 5 rows. After the 30 values have been read the B array looks like this:

3	8	9	7	2	4
15	0	6	0	1	8
1	3	8	9	3	1
0	12	13	10	16	4
8	4	0	8	12	3

Suppose we need the sums of all values in rows. That is, we need five sums, one for each row in the array. Here is how we may obtain them.

```
100   DIM B(5,6)

      ⋮ Additional Program Statements

150   FOR R = 1 to 5
160   LET S = 0
170   FOR C = 1 to 6
180   LET S = S + B(R,C)
190   NEXT C
200   PRINT S
210   NEXT R
220   END
```

How many sums does this program give?

421   30

422   5

FRAME 421

No, study the program. There is a loop within a loop. The inner loop is controlled by
C. The inner loop is executed six times and
<u>does</u> <u>not</u> have the statement

200   PRINT S

in it. (S means SUM in this example.) The
outer loop is controlled by R. That loop
<u>does</u> include the PRINT in it. The outer loop
is executed 5 times. Therefore, the PRINT
statement is executed 5 times and 5 sums are
printed.

Please go now to Frame 422.

FRAME 422

Five sums are printed.

At line 180 the B array employs two subscripts
R and C. The B element added to S is at the
intersection of the R row and the C column.
R and C are two subscripts for the array B.

You'll notice that this program uses a loop
within a loop. The inner loop extends from
lines 170 through 190 (FOR C to NEXT C). The
outer loop extends from lines 150 through 210
(FOR R to NEXT R).

The outer loop initializes R at 1, then sets
S to zero. Next it begins the inner loop by
setting C at 1 and cycling C through 6 in steps
of 1. While C cycles through 6, the value of
R remains at 1. Thus, the values added to S
as the inner loop cycles are: B(1,1); B(1,2);
B(1,3); B(1,4); B(1,5); and B(1,6).

The value of S is printed and the outer loop
cycles once more. This time R remains constant
at 2 while C cycles again from 1 to 6.

What values are added to S the second time S is
computed?

423   B(R,C) where R holds at 2 and C cycles
      from 1 through 6.

424   B (R,C) where R and C cycle from 1 to 6.

FRAME 423

Correct!

The correct answer is B (R,C) where R holds
at 2 and C cycles from 1 through 6.

Observe that memory cell S is reinitialized
to zero just before the inner loop cycles.

Let's study another example involving arrays.
Suppose we want to create the multiplication
table from 0 to 5 only. We want this:

	0	1	2	3	4	5
0	0	0	0	0	0	0
1	0	1	2	3	4	5
2	0	2	4	6	8	10
3	0	3	6	9	12	15
4	0	4	8	12	16	20
5	0	5	10	15	20	25

What is the size of this array?

425   25 memory cells

426   36 memory cells

427   5 memory cells

FRAME 424

No, your answer is not correct. Examine the
two loops carefully. The inner and outer
loops have this relationship:

```
          FOR R = 1 TO 5
                .
                .
                .
          FOR C = 1 TO 6
                .
                .
                .
          NEXT C
                .
                .
                .
          NEXT R
```

The PRINT S statement lies between NEXT C and
NEXT R. It will print only 5 times.

Considering this additional information, please
return to Frame 422 and make a better selection.

FRAME 425

No, your answer is off the mark. Count the
number of rows and columns. There are 6
each, not 5 as you might, at first, presume.

Please return to Frame 423 and make another
selection.

FRAME 426

You're right.   There are 36 memory cells.

To solve the given problem we can write the
program this way:

```
100   DIM T (6, 6)
110   FOR R = 1 to 6
120   FOR C = 1 to 6
130   LET T(R,C) = (R - 1) * (C - 1)
140   NEXT C
150   NEXT R
160   MAT PRINT T
170   END
```

Why does this program multiply (R - 1) by
(C - 1) instead of R by C?

428   (R - 1) * (C - 1) actually gives the
      same answer as R * C

429   The multiplication table has a zero row
      and a zero column, but zero rows and
      zero columns don't exist in BASIC arrays.

FRAME 427

No, your answer is not correct. There are
6 x 6 (36) memory cells. To obtain the answer you simply multiply the number of rows
(6) by the number of columns (6).

You appear to need a review. Please return
to Frame 410, then proceed from there.

FRAME 428

No, you appear to be guessing. When you multiply (R-1) by (C-1), the results you obtain
fall correctly into the table memory cells.
The tabulation in Frame 429 shows this clearly.

Please proceed to Frame 429.

FRAME 429

Right!

The multiplication table has a zero row and a zero column but zero rows and columns don't exist in BASIC arrays.

As the program runs, this is a summary of its action:

R (Row)	C (Column)	COMPUTED PRODUCT (R - 1) * (C - 1)
1	1	0
1	2	0
1	3	0
1	4	0
1	5	0
1	6	0
2	1	0
2	2	1
2	3	2
2	4	3
2	5	4
2	6	5
3	1	0
3	2	2
3	3	4
	etc.	

How many values are computed to establish the multiplication table?

430   36

431   25

432   900

FRAME 430

The answer is 36.

The MAT PRINT command is used to print out
the contents of an entire array. The dimension of the array is obtained from the DIM
statement.

Observe that in all the examples we've given
for two dimensional arrays, the row subscript
has always been R and the column subscript
has always been C. This was done as a matter
of convenience. You can give row subscripts
and column subscripts any names you please.

There is no reply required for this frame.
Congratulations for having successfully completed this section and the course. We hope
you enjoy programming in BASIC.

FRAME 431

No, there are 36 values needed to fill in
the 36 memory cells of the table. Therefore, the program will have an outer loop
which executes 6 times and an inner loop
which executes 6 times. The value for 2
x 4, for example, is stored in two places:
At the point where row is 2 and column is
4 and at the point where row is 4 and column
is 2. To compute the former, R's value must
be 5. To compute the latter, R's value must
be 5 and C's value must be 3.

Please proceed now to Frame 430.

FRAME 432

No, your response is not correct. Since there
are only 36 memory cells in the table, the
number 900 is much too large.

You appear to need a thorough review. Please
proceed to Frame 384 and continue from there.

SECTION I

QUIZ

1. Why is the word "conversational" used in the term "conversational timesharing?"

2. What should your response be when the computer asks: ID?

3. What should your response be when the computer asks: SYSTEM?

4. What should your response be when the computer asks: NEW OR OLD?

5. What does the computer ask for if you don't give a file name when responding to the question: NEW OR OLD?

6. How should you select a file name for a new program? That is, how do you decide what name to give when the computer asks for one?

7. What is a BASIC statement?

8. What is a line number?

9. What is a program?

10. When do you depress the RETURN key found on the keyboard of your terminal?

11. What are the 5 symbols used in BASIC which cause calculations to take place?

12. What does the RUN command do?

13. What does the SAVE command do?

14. What does the BYE command do?

15. Write a program that will assign 3.5 to X and 2.6 to Y, will cause the two values to be added, will assign the result to F, and will finally cause the value of F to be printed. (You will need three LET statements, a PRINT statement, and an END statement.)

16. Write a program that will assign 7.2 to A, -3.1 to Q, and 17.1 to R; will cause the three values to be added; will assign the result to G; then will cause the values of A, Q, R, and G to be printed.

17. Write a program that will assign 5.1 to M and 2.9 to N, will cause the two values to be multiplied, will assign the product to P, and will then cause M, N, and P to be printed.

18. Write a program that will assign 7 to H, and 6 to J, will cause H to be added to J, will assign the result to K, next will cause H to be multiplied by J, will assign the product to L, and will then cause H, J, K, and L to be printed. (You will need four LET statements, one PRINT statement, and one END statement.

SECTION I

QUIZ ANSWERS

1. Conversational timesharing is called "conversational" because the user and the computer engage in a give-and-take exchange when the user submits a job for the computer to process. The computer types something, then the user does, etc. until the job is defined.

2. When the computer requests your ID, give the ID assigned to you at the time you initially contracted for computer service.

3. When the computer requests the system identification, you should respond: BASIC.

4. When the computer asks NEW OR OLD, you should respond OLD if the job you wish to process is one created and saved at an earlier time. If the job to be run is a new one, then your response should be NEW.

5. If you don't give a file name when responding to the NEW OR OLD question, the computer will ask for a file name.

6. When you select a file name to be used

in association with a program, you should select a name that reminds you what the program does. Thus, if the program computes averages of grades, some good names might be AVGRDS, GRADAV, GRAVG, etc.

7. A BASIC statement is an instruction to the computer. The instruction is in the BASIC programming language and has three parts: line number, key word, and statement body.

8. A line number is an arbitrary identifying number for a BASIC statement. That number may be as small as "1" or as large as "99999".

9. A program is a set of instructions telling the computer what to do to find the solution of a given problem.

10. The RETURN key is depressed whenever you have finished entering a BASIC statement. The computer accepts the complete statement when you depress RETURN.

11. The five symbols used in BASIC to cause calculations to be made are: + (addition), - (subtraction), / (division), * (multiplication) and ↑ (exponentiation).

12. The RUN command is given when you want to have the computer execute (run) a program. The computer checks the program for obvious errors. If there are none, the program is executed.

13. The SAVE command is given when you want the computer to save a program you created. Having the name you gave it (for example AVGRDS), the program is saved for later use.

14. The BYE command is given when you
    have completed a session at the ter-
    minal and you wish to log off. Typ-
    ing BYE disconnects you from the com-
    puter.

15.   10   LET X = 3.5
             20   LET Y = 2.6
             30   LET F = X + Y
             40   PRINT F
             50   END

16.   10   LET A = 7.2
             20   LET Q = -3.1
             30   LET R = 17.1
             40   LET G = A + Q + R
             50   PRINT A, Q, R, G
             60   END

17.   10   LET M = 5.1
             20   LET N = 2.9
             30   LET P = M * N
             40   PRINT M, N, P
             50   END

18.   10   LET H = 7
             20   LET J = 6
             30   LET K = H + J
             40   LET L = H * J
             50   PRINT H, J, K, L
             60   END

SECTION II

QUIZ

1. What character do you employ when you want to correct errors on a character-by-character basis?

2. An assignment statement always begins with what key word?

3. What three types of information might you find on the right hand side of the equals sign (=) in an assignment statement?

4. In the assignment statement

        80   LET R = T + U

    what value is assigned to R if T's value is 8 and U's value is 35?

5. Why are parentheses used in assignment statements?

6. What is the upward arrow (↑) used for in assignment statements?

7. What is a BASIC variable name?

8. What are the rules for forming a BASIC variable name?

9. What is wrong with the variable name "7P"?

10. What is meant by the assignment state-ment

205 LET F = F + 6

11. Study this next program. Then tell what the computer will print as the values of A, B, C, and D.

```
10   LET A = 4
20   LET B = A + 2
30   LET C = A + 1
40   LET A = A + 1
50   LET D = B
60   PRINT A, B, C, D
70   END
```

12. Study this next program. Then tell the computer what it will print as the values of E, F, G, H, and I.

```
10   LET A = 5
20   LET B = 8
30   LET E = A + B
40   LET F = A - B
50   LET G = A * B
60   LET H = A / B
70   LET I = A ↑ 3
80   PRINT E, F, G, H, I
90   END
```

13. Write a program that will compute the value given by the expression

$$\frac{5}{10 + 5}$$

and will print the result.

14. Write a program that will compute the value given by the expression

$$\left[\frac{20 + 2}{10 - 6}\right]^5$$

and will print the result.

15. Write a program that will compute the value given by the expression

$$\left[\frac{2^{5.1}}{3^{2.1}}\right]^5 \quad X \quad \left[\frac{5^{4.1}}{2.7^3 + 1.8^5}\right]$$

QUIZ ANSWERS

1. The character used when making corrections on a character-by-character basis is the backwards arrow (←).

2. An assignment statement always begins with the key word LET.

3. The three types of information one may find on the right hand side of an equals sign in assignment statements are basic names, actual numeric values, and expressions.

4. The value assigned to R is 43.

5. In assignment statements parentheses are used to group values which are to be handled as units.

6. In assignment statements, the upward arrow (↑) is used to indicate exponentiation.

7. A BASIC variable name is a one or two-character label given to a numeric value. The name is termed "variable" because any value can be assigned to the name and that value can be changed by the program.

8. A variable name may be formed by a single
    letter of the alphabet (A, B, C, etc.)
    or by a single letter of the alphabet
    followed by a single digit (A5,C9, T5,
    etc.).

9. The variable name "7P" is wrong because
    a name may never begin with a digit.

10. The assignment statement causes the <u>old</u>
    value of F to be added to "6". The
    result to become the <u>new</u> value of F.

11. The values of A, B, C, and D are 5, 6,
    5, and 6, respectively.

12. The values of E, F, G, H, and I are 13,
    -3, 40, .625, and 125 respectively.

13.
```
        10   LET A = 5
        20   LET B = 10
        30   LET C = A / (B + A)
        40   PRINT C
        50   END
```

OR

```
        10   LET C = 5 / (10 + 5)
        20   PRINT C
        30   END
```

14.
```
    10   LET A = 20
    20   LET B = 2
    30   LET C = 10
    40   LET D = 6
    50   LET X = 5
    60   LET Y = ((A + B) / (C - D)) ↑ X
    70   PRINT Y
    80   END
```

OR

```
10   LET Y = ((20 + 2) / (10 - 6))↑5
20   PRINT Y
30   END
```

15.
```
 10   LET A = 2
 20   LET B = 3
 30   LET C = 5
 40   LET D = 2.7
 50   LET E = 1.8
 60   LET F = 5.1
 70   LET G = 2.1
 80   LET H = 4.1
 90   LET I = 3
100   LET J = (((A↑F)/(B↑G))↑C)*((C↑H)/
              (D↑I+E↑C))
110   PRINT J
120   END
```

OR

```
10   LET J = ((2↑5.1/3↑2.1)↑5)*(5↑4.1/
             (2.7↑3+1.8↑5))
20   PRINT J
30   END
```

NOTE: The first program contains a few
       extra sets of parentheses. While
       not actually needed, the extra
       parentheses do no harm.

SECTION III

QUIZ

1. What are the 5 symbols that cause arithmetic computations to take place?

2. When parentheses are not used in an expression what operations does a computer do first?

3. When parentheses are not used in an expression what operations does a computer do before additions and subtractions?

4. In the statement

        305   LET G = R * 5 ↑ 3 + B

    which calculation does the computer perform first?

5. In the statement in Question 4, which calculation does the computer perform last?

6. When you are in doubt concerning the use of parentheses, what is a good rule to follow?

7. What does the built in SIN function accomplish?

8. What is meant by the "argument" of a function?

453

9. Which of these functions is not built into BASIC

        SIN
        DET
        COS
        SQR
        LOG

10. What is the value assigned to G in the following statement:

    250   LET G = 6.5 + SQR(25)

11. Write the BASIC statement that will cause the following calculation to take place:

$$d = \left[\frac{\frac{8.5 + 5.7}{2.9}}{1.5 - 6.2} \right]^3$$

12. Write a program that will compute

$$\left[\frac{7^{3.1}}{2^5} \times 9^5 \right]^{7.3}$$

and will print the answer.

13. Write a program that will compute

$$\sqrt{9.5 \times 8.3}$$

and will print the answer.

14. Write a program that will compute

$$\sqrt{\sin (1.2) \times \cos (5.1)}$$

and will print the result.

15. Write a program that will compute the natural log of 6.1 + 7.2 and will print the result.

16. Study the following program. Tell what value the program will print.

```
10   LET X = SQR ((64/(3+5))+1)
20   PRINT X
30   END
```

QUIZ ANSWERS

1. The five symbols causing arithmetic computations to take place are + (add), - (subtract), / (divide), * (multiply), and ↟ (exponentiate).

2. When parentheses are not used in an expression, the computer does exponentiations first.

3. When parentheses are not used in an expression, the computer does multiplications and divisions ahead of additions and subtractions. The computer does exponentiations ahead of multiplications and divisions.

4. In the statement shown, the computer will perform 5 ↟ 3 first.

5. In the statement shown, the computer will add B to the result of R * 5 ↟ 3. This is the last operation performed.

6. When in doubt about using parentheses, a good rule is: If you're not sure that the computation will be correctly performed by leaving out the parentheses, but you are sure that it will be correctly performed by putting them in, then include the parentheses. More

simply stated, "when in doubt, put them in!"

7. The built in SIN function gives the sine of an angle when the angle is expressed in radian measure.

8. The argument of a function is the value which a function must be given in order to operate properly. For example, the argument needed for the SIN function is the angle expressed in radian measure.

9. All functions mentioned are built into BASIC except DET.

10. The value assigned to G in the given expression is

    $6.5 + \sqrt{25}$ or $6.5 + 5$ or 11.5

11. 10 LET D = (((8.5/2.9) + 5.7)/(1.5 - 6.2)) ↑ 3

12. 10 LET A = ((7↑3.1/2↑5) * 9↑5)↑7.3
    20 PRINT A
    30 END

13.   10 LET G = SQR(9.5 * 8.3)
       20 PRINT G
       30 END

14. 10 LET X = SQR(SIN(1.2) * COS(5.1))
    20 PRINT X
    30 END

15.   10 LET Q = LOG(6.1 + 7.2)
       20 PRINT Q
       30 END

16. The program will assign 3 to X, then print that value.

SECTION IV

QUIZ

1. Why is a PRINT statement useful in a program?

2. What does this PRINT statement accomplish?

    200   PRINT S,W,N

3. How many print zones are there on a sheet of output paper? What are the print positions?

4. What does this PRINT statement accomplish?

    235   PRINT "CHECK DATA"

5. What does this PRINT statement accomplish?

    274   PRINT

6. If the values of X and Y are 7.4 and -8.3, respectively, in what print positions will the "7" and the "8" print if the PRINT statement is

    1400   PRINT X,Y

7. What does the PRINT statement accomplish?

458

```
340   PRINT "VALUE OF P IS ";P
```

8. When would one type semicolons separating
    variable names (rather than commas) in a
    PRINT statement?

9. In BASIC, what does an IF statement accom-
    plish?

10. What are the 6 relational symbols used in
    an IF statement?

11. If an IF statement gives a condition that
    is true, where does the program jump to?

12. If an IF statement gives a condition that's
    false, what does the program do?

13. What are the 3 forms that values on both
    sides of the relational symbols in IF
    statements may have.

14. What's wrong with this IF statement?

    ```
    300   IF  6 < 7  THEN 800
    ```

15. Write a program which computes the area
    of a circular lens having a diameter of
    10 inches. The equation for computing
    area is A πr^2 where π has a value of
    3.1416 and r, the radius, is half the
    diameter. Have the program print the
    answer.

16. Write a program that will compute the
    gross pay of a person who worked 39.5
    hours at an hourly pay rate of $3.25.
    Have the program print the hours worked,
    the pay rate, and the gross pay.

17. Write a program that will compute 9% of
    $1600 and 10% of $1450 and will deter-
    mine which calculation will have the

larger yield.

18. Write a program that will compute the square root of 17.65, then will test the result to determine whether the result is greater than 4.2. If the answer is Yes, have the program compute the square root of 12 and print the result. If the answer is No, have the program compute the square root of 10 and print the result.

SECTION IV

QUIZ ANSWERS

1. A PRINT statement is useful in a program because it causes the computer to print on paper, so humans can see, what the computer has calculated.

2. The PRINT statement causes the value last assigned to S and W and N to be printed out.

3. There are 5 print zones on output paper. The print positions are 1-15, 16-30, 31-45, 46-60, and 61-75. Some terminals print only through print position 72.

4. The PRINT statement causes the literal message "CHECK DATA" to be printed beginning at print position 1.

5. The PRINT statement causes a single blank line to be provided.

6. The "7" in "7.4" will print in print position 2, and the "8" in "-8.3" will print in print position 17.

7. The PRINT statement causes the literal message "VALUE OF P IS" to print beginning at print position 1 and the value of P to be printed beginning at print position 16. If the value of P happens

461

to be -9.7, the minus sign will print
in print position 16; if the value of
P is 9.7, the "9" prints in print position 17.

8. One would use semicolons between variable names rather than commas if he
wishes the printed answers to be closer
together. When commas are used, only
5 values can be printed per line.
When semicolons are used, as many as
12 values can be printed per line.

9. In BASIC an IF statement causes a condition to be tested. The program then
jumps or continues in sequence depending upon whether the condition was
true or false.

10. The six relational symbols are =, >,
< , > =, < =, and <>. They mean equals,
greater than, less than, greater than
or equals, less than or equals, and
not equal.

11. If an IF statement gives a true condition, the program jumps to the line
number which follows the word THEN.

12. If an IF statement gives a false condition, the program goes to the statement which immediately follows the IF
statement.

13. On both sides of an IF statement, the
user may give a BASIC variable name,
an actual numeric value, or an expression.

14. The IF statement makes no sense. The
value "6" is always less than "7";
therefore, the program will always

jump to line 800. The IF statement
should actually be

```
300   GO TO 800
```

15.     ```
        10   LET A = 3.1416 * 5 * 5
        20   PRINT A
        30   END
```

<div align="center">OR</div>

```
        10   PRINT 3.1416 * 5 * 5
        20   END
```

16.     ```
        10   LET H = 39.5
        20   LET R = 3.25
        30   LET G = H * R
        40   PRINT H,R,G
        50   END
```

17.     ```
        10   LET X = .09 * 1600
        20   LET Y = .10 * 1450
        30   IF X > Y THEN 60
        40   PRINT ".10 * 1450 IS BETTER"
        50   GO TO 70
        60   PRINT ".09 * 1600 IS BETTER"
        70   END
```

<div align="center">OR</div>

```
        10   IF .09 * 1600 > .10 * 1450 THEN 40
        20   PRINT ".10 * 1450 IS BETTER"
        30   GO TO 50
        40   PRINT ".09 * 1600 IS BETTER"
        50   END
```

18.     ```
        10   LET P = SQR (17.65)
        20   IF P > 4.2 THEN 60
        30   LET A = SQR(10)
        40   PRINT A
        50   GO TO 80
```

```
60   LET A = SQR(12)
70   PRINT A
80   END
```

OR

```
10   LET P = SQR (17.65)
20   IF P > 4.2 THEN 60
30   LET A = SQR (10)
40   PRINT A
50   GO TO 80
60   LET A = SQR(12)
70   GO TO 40
80   END
```

OR

```
10   IF SQR(17.65) > 4.2 THEN 40
20   PRINT SQR(10)
30   GO TO 50
40   PRINT SQR(12)
50   END
```

SECTION V

QUIZ

1. Define the term "loop".

2. What are the four parts of a loop?

3. What is the function of a counter in a loop?

4. What is the function of a test-of-counter in a loop?

5. What is meant by the term "body of loop"?

6. Why is the counter in a loop incremented or decremented?

7. What two BASIC statement types are employed when loops are to be automated?

8. What does FOR accomplish in a loop?

9. What does NEXT accomplish in a loop?

10. What does STEP accomplish when used with a FOR statement?

11. What are the three forms that a beginning, ending, and step size value may have in a FOR statement?

12. Where does a program go after a loop has been completely executed?

13. What type of statement may one use in order to have the program exit from a loop before the loop is completely executed?

14. In a FOR statement what is the assumed step size, if a step size is not explicitly given?

15. Write a program that will cause the printer to print your name 100 times.

16. Write a program that will cause the printer to print on separate lines the numbers 1, 2, 3, 4, etc., through 20.

17. Write a program that will accomplish the same task as given in question 16, except that the square of each number will also be printed on the lines.

18. Study the next program. Identify the initialization of counter and augment-of-counter (increment or decrement).

```
10    PRINT "THIS PROGRAM SUMS ONE"
20    PRINT "HUNDRED DIGITS FROM ONE TO ONE"
30    PRINT "HUNDRED."
40    LET S = 0
50    LET C = 1
60    IF C > 100 THEN 100
70    LET S = S + C
80    LET C = C + 1
90    GO TO 60
100    PRINT S
110    END
```

19. Rewrite the program given in question 18 using FOR and NEXT statements.

20. Write a program that will compute a sine and cosine table for various values of N beginning at .1 and increasing through 6.3 in steps of .1. Use FOR and NEXT statements.

SECTION V

QUIZ ANSWERS

1. A loop is a series of statements in a
    program which are executed over and
    over, often thousands of times.

2. The four parts of a loop are initial-
    ization of counter, body of loop,
    incrementing or decrementing of
    counter, and testing of counter.

3. In a loop, a counter counts the num-
    ber of times that the statements in
    the loop have been executed.

4. In a loop, a test-of-counter checks
    the counter to determine whether the
    loop has been executed the required
    number of times.

5. In a loop, the body of the loop is
    that portion of the loop which gets
    executed over and over. The body of
    the loop may contain one statement
    or it may contain thousands.

6. In a loop the counter is incremented
    or decremented so that it may be pro-
    perly checked by the test-of-counter.
    Every time the loop is executed, the
    counter is either incremented or decre-
    mented.

7. When loops are to be automated the two
   statement types, which are used as a
   team, are FOR and NEXT.

8. In a loop, FOR tells the name of the
   counter, its initial value, its final
   value, and the step size, if any.

9. In a loop, NEXT tells where the statements in the body of a loop actually
   terminate. The FOR statement is placed
   at the beginning of the body of a loop
   and the NEXT statement is placed at the
   end.

10. In a FOR statement, STEP tells the value
    to be added to or subtracted from the
    loop's counter each time the loop is
    executed.

11. The three forms that beginning, ending,
    and step size values may have in a FOR
    statement are: an actual numeric value,
    such as 6; a BASIC variable name, such
    as T; and an expression, such as (P +
    D)/Q.

12. After a loop has been completely executed,
    the program will go directly to the
    statement that follows the NEXT statement.

13. If one wishes to have a program exit from
    a loop before the loop is completely
    executed, he may use the IF statement.

14. In a FOR statement when a step size is
    not explicitly given, the step size the
    computer assumes is 1.

15.
```
10   LET C = 1
20   IF C > 100 THEN 60
30   PRINT "JOHN ANDERSON"
```

```
40   LET C = C + 1
50   GO TO 20
60   END
```

OR

```
10   FOR C = 1 TO 100
20   PRINT "JOHN ANDERSON"
30   NEXT C
40   END
```

16.
```
10   LET N = 1
20   IF N > 20 THEN 60
30   PRINT N
40   LET N = N + 1
50   GO TO 20
60   END
```

OR

```
10   FOR N = 1 TO 20
20   PRINT N
30   NEXT N
40   END
```

17.
```
10   LET N = 1
20   IF N > 20 THEN 60
30   PRINT N, N ↑ 2
40   LET N = N + 1
50   GO TO 20
60   END
```

OR

```
10   FOR N = 1 TO 20
20   PRINT N, N ↑ 2
30   NEXT N
40   END
```

18.   The initialization of counter is

```
50   LET C = 1
```

The augment-of-counter is

```
80   LET C = C + 1
```

19. 10   PRINT "THIS PROGRAM SUMS ONE"
     20   PRINT "HUNDRED DIGITS FROM ONE TO ONE"
     30   PRINT "HUNDRED."
     40   LET S = 0
     50   FOR C = 1 TO 100
     60   LET S = S + C
     70   NEXT C
     80   PRINT S
     90   END

20.   10   FOR X = .1 TO 6.3 STEP .1
        20   PRINT X, SIN(X), COS(X)
        30   NEXT X
        40   END

SECTION VI

QUIZ

1. What is the function of a READ statement in a BASIC program?

2. What is the function of a DATA statement in a BASIC program?

3. What is the function of an INPUT statement in a BASIC program?

4. How does a person stop a program that is in an endless loop?

5. Where may a DATA statement appear in a BASIC program?

6. How many DATA statements may you have in a BASIC program?

7. When does the computer print OUT OF DATA?

8. What is a "sentinel value"?

9. How does one select a sentinel value to use in a DATA statement?

10. When would one use an INPUT statement in preference to a READ/DATA combination?

11. Write a program which sums these ten values in a DATA statement

    200   DATA 8, 4, 5, 9, 1, 2, 6, 14, 5, 7

    You may assume that it is known there are exactly 10 values in the DATA statement.

12. Write a program that will detect and print the smallest value in the same DATA statement as in question 11.

13. Write a program that will detect and print the smallest value and the largest value in the same DATA statement as in question 11.

14. Write a program that will find the average of the values in this next DATA statement:

    10   DATA 8, 2, 5, 14, 11, 6, 3, 999

    The value 999 is a sentinel that will detect the "end-of-file". The value is not to be used in computing the average. You may assume that it is known there are fewer than 100 values in the DATA statement.

15. Write a program that will print only the sixth number in this DATA statement.

    10   DATA 18, 20, 15, 5, 16, 18, 21, 45, 92

16. Write a program that will print only the value ahead of the sentinel value (-1000) in this next DATA statement:

    10   DATA 25, 918, 114, 21, 17, 19, 14, 499, -1000

You may assume that it is known there are fewer than 100 values in the DATA statement.

SECTION VI

QUIZ ANSWERS

1. In a BASIC program, the READ statement is used to obtain data values from an associated DATA statement.

2. The DATA statement in a BASIC program provides the values which are obtained by one or more READ statements in a program.

3. In a BASIC program, an INPUT statement is used to provide input values to the computer and differs from the READ statement in that the values are typed in by the user when they are required, and not obtained from the DATA statement.

4. A person may stop a program that is in an endless loop by depressing the BREAK key.

5. In a BASIC program, a DATA statement may appear anywhere as long as it precedes the END statement. There may, of course, be more than one DATA statement in a program.

6. There may be as many DATA statements in a program as the user wishes. If there are several DATA statements in a program, the computer treats them as if

they were one linked DATA statement.

7. The program prints OUT OF DATA when an attempt by a READ statement to obtain a data value fails, because all data values have been processed.

8. A sentinel value is a dummy value at the end of a DATA statement. The sentinel signals that the end of data values has been reached.

9. In selecting a sentinel value, one must be sure to select a value which cannot possibly turn up as an actual data value. The sentinel must be either much greater or much smaller than the actual values being used.

10. One would use an INPUT statement in preference to a READ/DATA combination when more interaction is needed between computer and user. Or if a person does not know what data values to supply until he has seen some results from trial values.

11.
```
10   LET S = 0
20   FOR C = 1 TO 10
30   READ V
40   LET S = S + V
50   NEXT C
60   PRINT S
200   DATA 8, 4, 5, 9, 1, 2, 6, 14, 5, 7
210   END
```

12.
```
10   READ L
20   FOR C = 1 TO 9
30   READ X
40   IF X < L THEN 60
50   GO TO 70
60   LET L = X
```

```
     70    NEXT C
     80    PRINT L
     200   DATA 8, 4, 5, 9, 1, 2, 6, 14, 5, 7
     210   END

13.  10    READ V
     20    LET L = V
     30    LET B = V
     40    FOR C = 1 TO 9
     50    READ X
     60    IF X < L THEN 90
     70    IF X > B THEN 110
     80    GO TO 120
     90    LET L = X
     100   GO TO 120
     110   LET B = X
     120   NEXT C
     130   PRINT L, B
     200   DATA 8, 4, 5, 9, 1, 2, 6, 14, 5, 7
     210   END

14.  10    DATA 8, 2, 5, 14, 11, 6, 3, 999
     15    LET S = 0
     20    FOR C = 1 TO 100
     30    READ X
     40    IF X = 999 THEN 70
     50    LET S = S + X
     60    NEXT C
     70    LET A = S/(C - 1)
     80    PRINT A
     90    END

15.  10    DATA 18, 20, 15, 5, 16, 18, 21, 45, 92
     15    FOR C = 1 TO 5
     20    READ X
     30    NEXT C
     40    READ X
     50    PRINT X
     60    END

16.  10    DATA 25, 918, 114, 21, 17, 19, 14, 499, -1000
     15    READ B
```

```
20   FOR C = 1 TO 100
30   READ X
40   IF X = -1000 THEN 70
50   LET B = X
60   NEXT C
70   PRINT B
80   END
```

SECTION VII

QUIZ

1. What is an array?

2. What does the DIM statement accomplish?

3. What is the rule concerning the naming of a working space in the computer memory?

4. What are the values found initially in all memory cells of a working area?

5. What is a subscript and what does it accomplish?

6. What are the three forms that a subscript may take?

7. If a program contains this statement

       10 DIM R(100)

   what are the values that subscripts may take in the program?

8. What is the maximum size that a working area in memory may have in a program?

9. May you have more than one array in any given program?

10. What three BASIC statements may be
     effectively employed to transfer
     numeric values from a DATA statement
     to a working area in memory?

11. Read these 10 values into an array
     named W. Then have the program print
     the values.

100 DATA 88, 42, 21, 23, 19, 17, 20, 15, 43, 75

12. Refer to Question 11. Read the 10
     values into an array W, then copy
     the values into an array named Y.
     Have the program print the Y values.

13. Refer to Question 11. Read the 10
     values into an array W, then copy
     the values in reverse order into an
     array named Z.

     (Problems 14 and 15 in this section
     are relatively difficult. Do not be
     concerned if you cannot work them
     out. Detailed explanations are given
     in Section VIII.)

14. Refer to Question 11. Read the 10
     values into an array W, then have
     the program find and print the small-
     est value in the array.

15. Refer to Question 11. Read the 10
     values into an array W, then have
     the program print the values in
     numerically increasing sequence.
     Assume that all the values in the
     DATA statement are less than 1000.

SECTION VII

QUIZ ANSWERS

1. An array is an arrangement of numeric values. The array may be visualized as having one or more dimensions.

2. The DIM statement sets aside memory space for array usage. The DIM statement also gives the name and size of the memory space.

3. An array (working space) name may consist of a single letter of the alphabet.

4. The values found initially in working space are zeroes.

5. A subscript is a pointer. The subscript defines which value in a working space is being accessed. A subscript may be: a numeric value, such as (58); a name, such as K3; or an expression such as (P-T)/5.

6. The three forms that a subscript may take are: numeric value; BASIC name; and expression (See answer to Question 5).

7. In the program, subscripts may range from 1 through 100, inclusive. Subscripts may not be less than 1, nor more

than 100. Subscripts must be whole numbers (integers). In BASIC, if a subscript contains a fractional part, the computer will drop the fractional part (truncate it) when applying it against an array.

8. The maximum size that any single array may have is 1023 cells.

9. You may have as many arrays in a program as you wish. (Recall that each one must have a unique name consisting of a single letter of the alphabet, thus limiting the number of arrays to 26.)

10. The three BASIC statements which may be effectively employed to transfer values from a DATA statement to an array are FOR, READ, and NEXT.

11.
```
10   DIM W(10)
20   FOR N = 1 TO 10
30   READ W(N)
40   NEXT N
50   FOR K = 1 TO 10
60   PRINT W(K)
70   NEXT K
100  DATA 88, 42, 21, 23, 19, 17, 20, 15, 43, 75
110  END
```

12.
```
10   DIM W(10), Y(10)
20   FOR N = 1 TO 10
30   READ W(N)
40   NEXT N
50   FOR Q = 1 TO 10
60   LET Y(Q) = W(Q)
70   NEXT Q
100  DATA 88, 42, 21, 23, 19, 17, 20, 15, 43, 75
110  FOR K = 1 TO 10
120  PRINT Y(K)
```

```
130   NEXT K
140   END
```

13.
```
10    DIM W(10), Z(10)
20    FOR I = 1 TO 10
30    READ W(I)
40    NEXT I
50    FOR J = 1 TO 10
60    LET Z(J) = W(11-J)
70    NEXT J
80    FOR K = 1 TO 10
90    PRINT Z(K)
100   DATA 88, 42, 21, 33, 19, 17, 20, 15, 43, 75
110   NEXT K
120   END
```

14.
```
10    DIM W(10)
20    FOR I = 1 TO 10
30    READ W(I)
40    NEXT I
50    LET S = W(1)
60    FOR J = 2 TO 10
70    IF S < W(J) THEN 90
80    LET S = W(J)
90    NEXT J
100   DATA 88, 42, 21, 23, 19, 17, 20, 15, 43, 75
110   PRINT S
120   END
```

15.
```
10    DIM W(10)
20    FOR E = 1 TO 10
30    READ W(E)
40    NEXT E
50    FOR M = 1 TO 10
60    LET S = W(1)
70    LET L = 1
80    FOR N = 2 TO 10
90    IF S < = W(N) THEN 130
100   DATA 88, 42, 21, 23, 19, 17, 20, 15, 43, 75
110   LET S = W(N)
120   LET L = N
130   NEXT N
```

```
140   LET W(L) = 1000
150   PRINT S
160   NEXT M
170   END
```

SECTION VIII

QUIZ

1. What three statements may be used most effectively when an array is being searched?

2. If an array is being searched for the smallest value, why is the first value of the array placed in a cell called S?

3. If an array is being searched, when will S's value change? (See question 2.)

4. If an array is to be searched for a given value, how may that value be efficiently entered into the program?

5. What is a two dimensional array?

6. In the statement

        10 DIM B (5,6)

   how many rows and columns does the working area B have?

7. In BASIC is it permissible to have a FOR/NEXT loop within another FOR/NEXT loop?

8. What does the MAT READ statement accomplish?

9. What does the MAT PRINT statement accomplish?

10. What are two ways that you may stop a
    program which repeatedly goes to an
    INPUT statement to obtain one or more
    input values?

11. Write a program that places these
    values into an array in reverse order

10 DATA 8, 7, 17, 4, 71, 43, 83, 3, 27, 35

    Then have the program print the values.
    Use only one array to solve the problem.

12. Write a program that establishes an
    array named W having a size of 20.
    Then have the program place the values
    2, 4, 6 2, 4, 6, -------- 40 into
    the array. Finally, have the pro-
    gram print the array.

13. Read these next values into a 4 x 4
    array. Then have the program sum
    only the values on the diagonals and
    print the sum.

10 DATA 4,12,8,3,6,4,1,18,19,3,24,7,9,5,13,15

14. Write a program that reads these next
    values into an array, then sorts them
    in increasing sequence, and prints the
    sorted values. Use only one array to
    solve the problem. Any method that
    solves the problem is acceptable.

10 DIM 56, 64, 14, 83, 8, 45, 21, 94, 36, 80

SECTION VIII

QUIZ ANSWERS

1. The three statements which may be effect-
    ively used when an array is being searched
    are FOR, NEXT, and IF.

2. If an array is being searched for the
    smallest value, the first value of the
    array is placed in a cell called S in
    order to establish an initial value for
    S against which other values may be com-
    pared.

3. In connection with Question 2, if an ar-
    ray is being searched, the value of S
    will change when a value smaller than S
    is found in the array.

4. If an array is to be searched for a given
    value, that value may be entered into
    the program via BASIC's INPUT statement.

5. A two dimensional array may be visualized
    as having both row and column dimensions.
    When a subscript is used in connection
    with the array, the array must show both
    row and column values. (See Question 6.)

6. In the statement, the number of rows in
    array B is 5 and the number of columns
    in the same array is 6.

7. In BASIC it is permissible for one FOR/NEXT loop to be programmed completely within another FOR/NEXT loop.

8. The MAT READ command in BASIC causes an entire array to be filled with data values, which were obtained from a DATA statement.

9. The MAT PRINT statement causes an entire array of values to be printed.

10. There are two ways that a program, which obtains values from an INPUT statement, may be terminated. The first is to depress the BREAK key when the computer types a question mark. The second is to enter a sentinel value which the computer tests for after it has been entered (with an IF statement).

11.
```
10   DATA 8, 7, 17, 4, 71, 43, 83, 3, 27, 35
20   DIM A(10)
30   FOR N = 1 TO 10
40   READ A(N)
50   NEXT N
60   FOR N = 1 TO 5
70   LET T = A(N)
80   LET A(N) = A(11-N)
90   LET A(11-N) = T
100   NEXT N
110   FOR P = 1 TO 10
120   PRINT A(P)
130   NEXT P
140   END
```

12.
```
10   DIM W(20)
20   FOR J = 1 TO 20
30   LET W(J) = 2 * J
40   NEXT J
```

```
50    FOR K = 1 TO 20
60    PRINT W(K)
70    NEXT K
80    END
```

13.
```
10    DATA 4,12,8,3,6,4,1,18,19,3,24,7,9,5,13,15
20    DIM X(4,4)
30    MAT READ X
40    LET S = 0
50    FOR T = 1 TO 4
60    LET S = S + X(T,T)
70    LET S = S + X(T,5-T)
80    NEXT T
90    PRINT S
100   END
```

14.
```
10    DATA 56, 64, 14, 83, 8, 45, 21, 94, 36, 80
20    DIM A(10)
30    FOR  L = 1 TO 10
40    READ  A(L)
50    NEXT  L
60    FOR  I = 1 TO 9
70    LET  F = 0
80    FOR  J = 1 TO 10-I
90    IF   A(J) <= A(J+1) THEN 140
100   LET   T = A(J)
110   LET   A(J) = A(J+1)
120   LET   A(J+1) = T
130   LET   F = 1
140   NEXT J
150   IF   F = 0 THEN 170
160   NEXT  I
170   FOR  N = 1 TO 10
180   PRINT A(N)
190   NEXT N
200   END
```

GLOSSARY

Absolute Value: The positive form of any given number. Thus the absolute value of 187 is 187 and the absolute value of -96 is 96.

ALGOL: A computer programming language. Useful for scientific problem solving.

Array: A set of values arranged in a regular pattern such as in single-file or in two dimensions.

Assignment Statement: A BASIC statement that begins with the word LET. The value that is shown on the right hand side of the equal sign is stored in the name given on the left hand side.

BASIC: A computer programming language. Useful for scientific and business problem solving.

BASIC Statement: See Statement.

Body of Statement: The main part of a BASIC statement; the part that immediately follows the key word.

Break Key: A key on the keyboard of your terminal that may be used to stop a program which appears to be in a loop.

490

Cell: See Memory Cell.

Computer: An electronic device used for making calculations and for processing business data. Two of a computer's most impressive characteristics are extremely high processing speeds and very large memory capacities.

Conditional Statement: A statement that requires a test to be made. An IF statement is a conditional statement since the computer will take one of two alternate paths.

Cosine: In a right triangle, the value obtained when the side adjacent to an angle is divided by the hypothenuse.

Conversational Timesharing: See Timesharing.

Data: The input values that a computer must have in order to solve a given problem.

Data Name: A BASIC name having one or two characters to which a value can be assigned.

Decrement: To decrease the value of a counter.

Dimension: The number of elements in an array and their configuration (one or two dimensions). In BASIC, the DIM statement gives the dimensions of an array.

Disk: See Magnetic Disk.

e: A never ending number used in mathematics. The first few digits of the number are 2.718 281828.

Exponentiation: Raising a value to some power. Thus,

$$100 \quad LET \ R = W \uparrow 5$$

is the same as

$$100 \quad LET \ R = W * W * W * W * W$$

Expression: In an assignment statement, the value to the right of the equal sign.

File: A collection of data to be used with a computer program. The program itself is often called a file.

Flowchart: A pictorial representation of what you want the computer to do and in what sequence.

Flowcharting: The process of developing a flowchart.

FORTRAN: A computer programming language. Useful for scientific problem solving.

ID: Your personal identification validating your right to use a distant computer in time sharing mode.

Increment: To increase the value of a counter.

Information: The output given by a computer program. The answers to the problem.

Initialization: Giving first values to a data name. In loops, counters are normally initialized to 1.

Input: The values that a program must have in order to solve a given problem. See also Data.

Integer: A whole number.

Key Word: In BASIC, the first word of a statement that identifies the type of state-

ment.   Some key words are LET, IF, GO TO,
PRINT, etc.

Line Number: An identifying number that is
placed ahead of each BASIC statement in a
program.

Log (Base 10):   The value to which 10 must
be raised in order to obtain a given value.
(The base 10 log of 100 is 2.)

Log (Natural):   The value to which "e" must
be raised in order to obtain a given value.
(The natural log of 1 is 0.)

Log-on Procedure: The questions and answers
between a distant computer and the user that
validates the user and permits him to begin
using the computer.

Loop: A set of statements that are executed
over and over.

Magnetic Disk: Computer hardware upon which
programs and/or data files may be stored.

Matrix: An arrangement of related values
either in one or two dimensions.

Memory: A computer can store electronically
within its mechanism several million characters of information at any given moment. In
back up devices, computers can store up to
several trillion characters for relatively
immediate use.

Memory Cell: A unit in the memory of a computer capable of holding one or more characters of data.   A memory cell can also hold
numeric values.

Output: The answers given by a computer
program.   See also Information.

Permanent Storage Space: A place in a computer system, usually a magnetic disk, where your programs can be stored for a given length of time.

Print: To print answers on the output paper available with your terminal.

Processing Speed: A computer can do as much computing, and other data processing, in one second as a person can do in one year.

Program: A set of instructions telling a computer how to solve a given problem. The instructions are given in a programming language such as BASIC.

Programmer: A person who develops computer programs.

Programming: The process of developing a computer program.

Read: To obtain data from a DATA statement.

Relational Symbols: The symbols >, =, and < that may be used to indicate whether one value is larger, smaller, equal, or not equal to another. Relational symbols are used in IF statements.

Return Key: A key on your terminal's keyboard that you use to enter a BASIC statement you have typed.

Search: The finding of a particular value in a table or array.

Sentinel Value: A value found in a DATA

statement that signals the end of the data values.

Sine: In a right triangle, the value obtained when the side opposite the angle is divided by the hypothenuse.

Square Root: The number which, when multiplied by itself gives a given number. Thus, the square root of 64 is 8.

Statement: A single instruction to the computer such as

$$10 \quad LET \ P = 42.6$$

Step Size: The value by which a counter of a loop is changed.

Subscript: A number, name, or expression that tells which one of an array element is to be worked with.

System Command: A command directly to the computer telling it to do something with a program you have created or wish to create. Some system commands are SAVE, UNSAVE, LIST, RUN, NEW, OLD. BYE is also a system command that disconnects you from the distant computer.

Table: See Array.

Tangent: In a right triangle, the value obtained when the side opposite the angle is divided by the side adjacent to the angle.

Terminal: A device looking like a teletype or a typewriter on a large stand. Through it a user can gain access to a distant computer and converse with the computer to solve a given problem.

Test: To check out, such as the value of
a counter, the state of a condition, a
program, etc.

Timesharing: A method of using a computer
by means of the telephone. This system
allows many people to be connected to the
distant computer at the same time. The
computer shares its time among all users.

Variable Name: See data name.

Working Area: A place in the computer's
memory where you can work with arrays.

Working Space: A place in a computer
where you can work with programs.

Zone: One of the five areas on the terminal output paper where an answer may be
printed.

* means multiply   page 63
/   — divide   ——— 92

INDEX

502

page

44 KEY WORDS (14)

52 SYMBOLS, ARITHMETIC

67-68 ← BACKWARDS ARROW

101 ↑ RAISED TO A POWER (EXPONENTIATION)